The
BEST
is
YET
to
COME

WHAT THE BIBLE
SAYS ABOUT HEAVEN

The BEST *is* YET *to* COME

WHAT THE BIBLE
SAYS ABOUT HEAVEN

BY

Diane M. Kannady

TruCONNECTIONS
PRESS

Published by TruConnections Press   ISBN 13: 978-0-9846967-5-8

DEDICATION

This book is dedicated to the Riches in Christ family. Without your love, friendship, prayers and support, this book would not have been possible. Thank you.

May our hunger to know God more fully and to represent Him more accurately be ever increasing.

CONTENTS

PREFACE: WHY A BOOK ABOUT HEAVEN?

We all have one thing in common: we're going to die. This certainty leads to an inevitable question. What is beyond the grave? This book arises out of my own search over a number of years for answers to that question. What I discovered has been life changing for me. I think it will be for you also.

As a Christian, I believe in life after death and the hope of Heaven. But there's not much information out there about our eternal home. What little is said makes Heaven sound rather uninviting—a place with harps and clouds where people no longer recognize each other. I've read a number of books written by men and women who claim to have visited Heaven. Honestly, they weren't very helpful. Some I enjoyed, some I found to be silly, while others contradicted basic tenets of the Christian faith. Contemporary preaching doesn't provide much help either because most sermons emphasize how to make this life the best it can be with practically no reference to what happens when we die.

So I determined to find out from the Bible what life after death will be like. I had previously heard people say that there's very little about Heaven in the Bible. But that's not the case. The more I looked, the more I found. I wrote this book because I want to share with others some of the plentiful and beneficial information I gleaned from God's Word about the life to come. Before we get to it, let me give you some brief guidelines about the book that will help you get maximum benefit as you read.

First, by devoting an entire book to the subject of life after this life, I'm not suggesting that this life is unimportant. By all means, live the best life you can now. Dream big! Set goals!

Achieve those dreams and goals as best you can! But also keep in mind that the majority of your existence comes after this life. Humans are eternal beings who don't cease to exist at death. Therefore, even if we live to be one hundred years old, it's infinitesimal in comparison to forever. If we don't learn to live with the awareness that there's more to life than just this life, this very challenging world will be much more difficult for us. And we'll be robbed of the joy that comes from anticipating what's next in the life to come. My aim in writing this book is to help you develop a new perspective and begin to see your life in terms of eternity as you endeavor to live this life to the fullest.

Second, this book is laid out in a purposeful, systematic way. Heaven must be understood in the context of the overall plan of God. Consequently, I have weaved information about our eternal home with statements about the Lord's purpose in creating humankind and the earth. I introduce concepts in the opening chapters that are increasingly expanded upon as the book unfolds. This means you'll encounter information early on that won't be discussed in detail until later in the book, so you may be left wanting more. Be patient and stick with it because a fuller discussion awaits you in the second half of the book. Because the book progresses systematically, skipping over chapters to get to ones that sound more interesting may not be helpful. Each chapter is written on the basis of what I've discussed in the previous pages.

Third, this book isn't an exhaustive study. Part of my goal was to keep the book as short as possible. This means that I haven't addressed every issue connected with life in Heaven. And some topics could be discussed in greater detail. Neither do I attempt to answer every question that might arise about Heaven. But I've tried to deal with the most common ideas and concerns people voice about life after death. I believe

I've included enough information that, by the time you've finished reading this brief volume, you will have a hope and an excitement about what's ahead, even if every question can't be answered yet.

Fourth, as you read, you will notice that I occasionally refer to the original meanings of certain words and that I cite a number of different Bible translations. The Bible was not written in English. The authors wrote in Hebrew (the Old Testament) and in Greek (the New Testament). Through the centuries, the Scripture has been translated into other languages, including English. The best known English translation is the King James Version (KJV). This is the one I most often read and use in my studies. However, the KJV was translated in AD 1611 and the English language has changed a lot since then. We no longer use many words that were common in the 1600s, and the meanings of other words have changed. It is therefore sometimes necessary to examine original Greek and Hebrew wordings in order to clarify passages in the KJV. It is also helpful to consult other translations that utilize updated wordings and are more consistent with modern English while remaining true to the original Hebrew and Greek languages. Additionally, all scriptures have been formatted in italics so that they stand out, and certain words and passages within the scriptures have been emphasized using bold lettering.

Lastly, you will find a number of places where I direct the reader to look at notes with additional information on specific points. These notes are located at the back of the book.

$\mathcal{I}$NTRODUCTION

Although we might not want to admit it, most of us aren't that excited about going to Heaven. If we're brutally honest, the greatest attraction of Heaven is that it's not Hell. After all, who really wants to live on a cloud and play a harp forever, even if the cloud has a mansion and a golden street on it? Few of us look forward to spending eternity singing and worshipping in an unending church service. And the thought of not being able to recognize our loved ones makes Heaven even more uninviting. On top of that, does anybody truly want to leave this beautiful world behind? Of course, we'll be glad to get rid of the hardships and troubles of life. But the idea that we'll never sit beside a mountain stream, see another sunrise, or feel a summer breeze on our face is so disheartening.

Happily, every one of these statements regarding life in Heaven is contrary to what the Bible reveals. In this book, we are going to examine what God's Word says about Heaven. Where is it? What is it like? Why should you be excited about going? Lack of accurate information regarding our eternal home has robbed many people of what should be a source of great hope and joy: we're going to Heaven and the greater and better part of our existence is ahead!

The Bible records the accounts of men who visited our future home. Their testimonies of what they saw and heard reveal that the best is yet to come for those who know the Lord. One of those men is the great apostle Paul, an early follower of Jesus. He was taken to Heaven many years before he died. When he was later imprisoned and facing possible execution for his faith, he wrote, *"For to me, to live is Christ and **to die*** *is gain...I desire to depart and be with Christ, which is **better by far**"* (Philippians 1:21-23, NIV). Paul had no fear of death because he knew his best days were ahead of him. People often speak of life after this life as the afterlife. But that's a mistake. This present life is the *pre-life.*

It's sometimes said of those who have died that they're in a better place. Unfortunately, because of misinformation about Heaven, this powerful reality has been watered down to little more than a religious platitude. *Better* means "superior and thus more advantageous," nothing like the common ideas many individuals have about Heaven (*Webster's New Students Dictionary* 1969). Paul knew from his own experience that life in Heaven is better. According to a man who'd been there, it surpasses this life because it's all gain.

The Bible has much to say about what awaits us when we die. Heaven is a real place with real people who do real things. Many objects and activities on earth are patterned after those in Heaven, giving us a glimpse of what Heaven looks like and how men and women live. Even though God's Word doesn't answer every question about life after death, it gives us enough information that we can be certain what lies ahead is better. Heaven is *gain, not loss, and the best is yet to come.*

PART ONE:

THE PRESENT HEAVEN

HEAVEN IS A REAL PLACE

*M*any struggle with the thought of going to Heaven because it doesn't seem real. It seems otherworldly. We can't see or touch it and our body doesn't come with us when we go. But Heaven isn't a ghostly realm populated with transparent beings. It's a real place.

We can't touch or see Heaven, not because it's unreal or less real than this world, but because it's in another dimension. Human beings live in a space-time continuum made up of physical matter perceived through our five senses. But there's more to reality than what we see, hear, touch, smell, or taste. Recent discoveries in quantum physics have led scientists to conclude that there are ten observable dimensions beyond the three that are discernible to people—length, width, and height (Missler and Eastman 1997, pp. 85-86).

AN UNSEEN WORLD

Science is beginning to confirm what the Bible has told us for centuries: there's an unseen realm—a dimension not normally visible to men and women on earth (2 Corinthians

4:18; Colossians 1:16). God's Word records a number of instances where this realm briefly opened to individuals and they were permitted to see the invisible world. Let's examine two of them.

Angelic Protectors

The first instance dates back over twenty-eight hundred years. The leader of Syria initiated a military campaign against the kingdom of Israel. Almighty God revealed Syria's secret battle plans to the great Hebrew prophet Elisha, which gave Israel a strategic advantage. When the Syrian king's advisors made him aware of the situation, he sent soldiers to capture the prophet at the Israeli city of Dothan (2 Kings 6:8-23).

Elisha's servant rose up early one morning to attend to his daily chores and was terrified to find the city surrounded by an enemy army. Elisha, however, was unafraid because he knew he was protected by beings in the invisible dimension—he had actually seen them in an earlier encounter. The prophet prayed and asked the Lord to open the young man's eyes so he could see their protectors.

> "[Then]...*the LORD opened the servant's eyes, and he looked and saw the hills full of horses and chariots of fire all around Elisha"* (2 Kings 6:17, NIV).

Elisha and his servant saw real horses and chariots. The chariots and animals had the appearance of fire, not because they were made of flames, but because they reflected the glorious light of the unseen realm.

Angelic Messengers

The second incident occurred the night Jesus was born into this world two millennia ago. As shepherds tended their flocks in a field near the town of Bethlehem, an angel came out of the heavenly dimension and announced the Lord's arrival. The angel was soon joined by a multitude of angels who were praising God. After these beings delivered their message, the opening between the visible and invisible realm closed.

> *"Suddenly, an angel of the Lord appeared among them, and the radiance of the Lord's glory surrounded them. [He said] 'I bring you good news of great joy for everyone! The Savior—yes, the Messiah, the Lord— has been born tonight in Bethlehem'...Suddenly, the angel was joined by a vast host of others—the armies of heaven—praising God: 'Glory to God in the highest heaven, and peace on earth to all whom God favors.' [Then] the angels...returned to heaven"* (Luke 2:9-15, NLT).

In both of these encounters, an invisible world was revealed to men on earth and they were able to perceive what had previously been imperceptible. These visitors from Heaven— angelic beings and horses with chariots—didn't suddenly come into existence when Elisha, his servant, and the shepherds saw them. They had been there all along. They were merely in a different dimension.

HEAVEN IS A LOCALITY

Heaven is not made of fluffy, see-through clouds. It's a real, tangible place. Jesus said so. He should know since He came from this unseen kingdom (John 3:13; John 6:38). Consider a

21

statement the Lord made as He spoke to His twelve disciples the night before He was crucified. His words reveal the reality of the invisible dimension.

> *"Let not your heart be troubled: ye believe in God, believe also in me. In my Father's house are many mansions: if it were not so, I would have told you. I go to prepare a **place** for you. And if I go and prepare a **place** for you, I will come again, and receive you unto myself; that where I am, there ye may be also"* (John 14:1-3, KJV).

Jesus was about to return to Heaven and leave this group of men whom He'd had daily contact with for three and a half years. His words were intended to bring them comfort and to encourage them that their impending separation was temporary. Eventually, they would all be reunited. The Lord assured them that He'd prepare a place for them in His Father's home. *Webster's New Students Dictionary* (1969) defines *place* as a "location in space." Jesus was returning to an actual locality where His disciples would one day join Him.

Some use this verse to say that in Heaven, we'll each have a huge mansion—a palace built of marble or granite or some other fine material, decorated with gold and precious stones. This idea can actually add to the unattractiveness of our future home because such a structure doesn't appeal to many of us. But Jesus never said we'd have a massive home. *Mansion* comes from a Greek word meaning "to dwell or remain" (Strong 2004). The Lord Jesus was making the point that there's plenty of room in His Father's house, and He and all of His followers can be together there. *"In my Father's house are many rooms"* (John 14:2, NIV); *"many dwelling places [homes]"* (John 14:2, AMP).

HEAVEN HAS SUBSTANCE

Even though Heaven is presently invisible to us, it has substance and materiality. God's home is so real that at least three men with physical bodies are able to live there. Jesus currently lives in the unseen realm in the same physical body He had while on earth. Following His death on the Cross, His lifeless remains were placed in a tomb. Three days later, Jesus rose from the dead. According to the Bible, people were able to see and touch the Lord after He was restored to life. They heard Him talk and saw Him eat. And they witnessed our Savior take this substantive, material body into Heaven forty days after His resurrection.

"While they [His disciples] *were still talking about this* [reports that the risen Lord was appearing to people], *Jesus himself stood among them and said to them, 'Peace be with you.' They were startled and frightened, thinking they saw a ghost. He said to them, 'Why are you troubled, and why do doubts rise in your minds? Look at my hands and my feet. It is I myself!* **Touch me and see; a ghost does not have flesh and bones, as you see I have.'** *When he had said this, he showed them his hands and feet"* (Luke 24:36-40, NIV).

"And while they still did not believe it because of joy and amazement, he asked them, 'Do you have anything here to eat?' **They gave him a piece of broiled fish, and he took it and ate it in their presence"** (Luke 24:41-43, NIV).

"[Forty days later] *when he* [Jesus] *had led them out of the vicinity of Bethany, he lifted up his hands and* *blessed them. While he was blessing them, **he left them and was taken up into heaven**"* (Luke 24:50-51, NIV).

Within months of the Lord's return to His Father's heavenly home, a man named Stephen was stoned to death for his faith in Christ. He became the first martyr among Jesus' followers. As Stephen's killers pummeled him with rocks, the veil that separates the invisible dimension from the visible world was momentarily pulled back and Stephen saw Jesus in Heaven.

"But Stephen, full of the Holy Spirit, looked up to heaven and saw the glory of God, and Jesus standing at the right hand of God. 'Look,' he said, 'I see heaven open and the Son of Man standing at the right hand of God'" (Acts 7:55-56, NIV).

Notice that Jesus was not transparent or ghostly and He wasn't floating on a cloud. He was in His physical body, standing to the right of God's throne. Stephen looked into a dimension with substance and spatial relationship between objects—the realm he entered when he drew his last breath.

That's Not the Only Physical Body in Heaven

The Bible reports that there are others in the unseen kingdom with material bodies. These men bypassed physical death and were taken directly into Heaven where they now live.

- Enoch, a man who walked with God throughout his life, entered Heaven with his physical body *"[when] suddenly, he disappeared because God took him"* (Genesis 5:24, NLT). *"**Enoch was taken up to heaven without dying**"*

(Hebrews 11:5, NLT).

- The Hebrew prophet Elijah also went into Heaven without experiencing death. His fellow prophet and protégé Elisha witnessed what happened: *"As they* [Elijah and Elisha] *were walking along and talking, suddenly a chariot of fire appeared, drawn by horses of fire. It drove between them, separating them, and **Elijah was carried by a whirlwind into heaven. Elisha saw it"** (2 Kings 2:11-12, NLT). This is why Elisha had no fear when he was surrounded by an enemy force in the incident mentioned earlier in the chapter.

There are human beings with physical bodies in Heaven right now. Yet we never see an occasional foot or hand sticking out through the clouds since Heaven is a real place with substance, tangibility, and materiality. Just because we can't see the unseen realm doesn't mean it's not real. Our future home is simply located in another dimension presently beyond the perception of our five physical senses.

God's Word records the testimony of men who entered the unseen world and then returned to earth to report what they witnessed. In the next chapter, we'll begin to examine what they saw and heard while in Heaven.

MEN HAVE VISITED HEAVEN

The Bible relates accounts of two men who each briefly visited Heaven—the apostles Paul and John. Their words provide insight into what our future home is like. Both men reveal that, although there are aspects of this unseen realm that can't be described, much of it is familiar because earth is patterned after heavenly realities. Just as God made man in His image, He made the earth in the image of Heaven. Let's look at some of what Paul and John reported.

PAUL IN HEAVEN

In a letter written to Christians living in the Greek city of Corinth, Paul disclosed that he had been caught up, or taken away, into Heaven a number of years earlier. He wrote that Heaven is so real he couldn't tell if he was in or out of his physical body.

> *"I know a man in Christ who fourteen years ago—whether in the body I do not know, or out of the body I do not know, God knows—such a man was caught up to the third heaven...into Paradise and heard in-*

expressible words, which a man is not permitted to speak" (2 Corinthians 12:2-4, NASB).

The apostle said he entered the third heaven. The religious scholars of his day spoke of three heavens. They called the atmosphere around them the first heaven. The second heaven was what we know as outer space. The third heaven was God's home. Paul also referred to it as Paradise.

Although Paul was instructed not to give specific details about his time in God's home, the reality of his experience permeates his writings (see note 1). Remember, he is the one who, while facing death, wrote that *"to die is gain"* because life is better in Heaven. This man also revealed that the physical, material creation around us provides information about the Lord and the invisible realm.

> *"There are things about him* [God] *that people cannot see—his eternal power and all the things that make him God. But since the beginning of the world those things have been easy to understand by what God has made"* (Romans 1:20, NCV).

Obviously, the grandeur of creation reveals something of the power and majesty of Almighty God. However, according to the Bible, there are objects and activities on earth that resemble those in Heaven, giving us a window into this unseen world. As noted in the previous chapter, when the invisible dimension opened to Elisha's servant and the shepherds at Bethlehem, they saw and heard things familiar and recognizable, such as chariots, horses, and intelligible words of worship and praise to God.

Paul further reported that a building known to the people

of his day—the magnificent Temple that stood in the city of Jerusalem—was patterned after a structure in Heaven. He called the earthly structure *"a place of worship that is only a copy, a shadow of the real one in heaven"* and said that *"everything in it...were copies of things in heaven"* (Hebrews 8:5; Hebrews 9:23, NLT). The apostle Paul didn't say whether or not he saw this heavenly Temple while he was in Heaven, but John wrote that he saw it (Revelation 7:15; Revelation 11:19; Revelation 15:5) (see note 2).

JOHN IN HEAVEN

John was one of Jesus' original twelve disciples. Sixty years after Jesus returned to Heaven (about AD 95), the Lord appeared to John on the island of Patmos, which is off the coast of modern-day Turkey. He gave John messages for seven churches located in the region at that time. Our Savior then took John into Heaven where he received the information he recorded in the Book of Revelation (Revelation 1:19).

John's writings describe what will happen in Heaven and on earth in the last few years leading up to the Second Coming of Christ. Although Revelation wasn't written to give a detailed description of daily life in the invisible realm, we learn much about it through what John witnessed. John observed a number of items and activities in Heaven that are also found on earth.

> *"Then as I looked, I saw a **door** standing open in heaven, and the same voice I had heard before spoke to me with the sound of a mighty trumpet blast...and I saw a **throne** in heaven and someone **sitting** on it... Twenty-four **thrones** surrounded him, and twenty-four elders **sat** on them. They were all **clothed in white** and had **gold crowns** on their **heads**...the twenty-four el-*

*ders **fall down and worship** the one who lives forever and ever. And they **lay their crowns** before the throne and say, 'You are worthy, O Lord our God'"* (Revelation 4:1-4; Revelation 4:10, NLT).

*"And I saw a **scroll** in the right hand of the one sitting on the throne. There was **writing** on the inside and the outside of the scroll, and it was sealed with seven **seals**"* (Revelation 5:1, NLT).

"Each one [the elders] *had a **harp**, and they held **gold bowls** filled with **incense**—the prayers of God's people! And they **sang** a new **song**...And then I heard **every creature** in heaven and on earth and under the earth and in the sea. They also **sang**"* (Revelation 5:8-9; Revelation 5:13, NLT).

*"After this I saw a vast crowd, too great to count, from every nation and tribe and people and language, **standing** in front of the throne and before the Lamb. They were **clothed in white** and held **palm branches** in their **hands**"* (Revelation 7:9, NLT).

Don't miss the impact of John's words. He reported that in Heaven he saw a door, furniture (thrones or chairs), clothing (robes), jewelry (crowns), a book with writing (scroll), musical instruments (harps), bowls, incense, and palm branches (from either trees or plants). He heard songs and singing and witnessed people with heads and hands moving around with much activity. The apostle saw animals. The Greek word translated *creature* means "living thing" and is used elsewhere in the New Testament to refer to animals (Hebrews 13:11; 2 Peter 2:12; Jude 10) (Strong 2004).

John, like Paul, discovered that Heaven has physicality. John wrote that while in the invisible dimension, he had a body with a mouth and a belly. He grasped and held objects. He ate and tasted things.

> *"So I approached him* [an angel] *and asked him to give me the little scroll* [another book]. *'Yes, take it and eat it,' he said. 'At first it will taste like honey, but when you swallow it, it will make your stomach sour!' So **I took** the little scroll from the hands of the angel, and **I ate** it! It was sweet in **my mouth**, but it made **my stomach** sour"* (Revelation 10:9-10, NLT).

At the end of his vision, John watched the capital city of Heaven come down to earth. We'll examine this in greater detail in Chapter 9, but the fact that there's a city in the unseen realm that can also exist on earth is another indication of the physicality of Heaven. It's a place of substance. The apostle reported that proportion and dimension exist in this heavenly metropolis. The city has four sides—east, west, north, south—as well as length, width, and height. The capital has the attributes of earthly cities, including architecture, walls with foundations, gates, streets, rivers, and trees. John went on to describe pearls and other precious minerals, such as sapphires, emeralds, onyx, and topaz—all items found here on earth.

A GARDEN, A COUNTRY, A CITY

Paul and John both had some understanding of Heaven before they visited there. They had gleaned information from the Old Testament, the portion of the Bible completed by their day. We'll look more closely at what the Old Testament reveals about Heaven in the second half of this book. Note one point now.

I mentioned earlier that Paul called the place he visited Paradise. He wasn't being poetic with his word choice. Paradise was a common name for the home of the righteous dead in his day. The term comes from the Greek word *paradeisos*, meaning "park or garden" (Strong 2004). Greek was the language most frequently spoken at that time, and when the Old Testament was first translated from Hebrew into Greek, *paradeisos* was used for the Garden of Eden (Genesis 2:8; Ezekiel 28:13). First-century people expected Heaven to be a paradise like Eden.

Since earth is patterned after heavenly realities, it's reasonable to conclude that Eden, God's original home for mankind, provides details about our future residence. The opening pages of the Bible describe the Garden as a beautiful place of full provision with trees, plants, and food. There were animals, rivers, minerals, and gold. The first human beings, Adam and Eve, engaged in meaningful work and had close interaction with each other and the Lord (Genesis 2). As we delve deeper into what the Scripture reveals about Heaven, we'll find that all of these elements are part of the life that awaits us.

Paul further recorded that followers of God who lived before him believed they were headed not only for a garden but for a city and a country in the life to come. He wrote that *"they desire a better country, that is, a heavenly one"* (Hebrews 11:16, NASB). "[They were] *looking forward to* [their] *city in heaven, which is yet to come"* (Hebrews 13:14, NLT). Each of these terms draws up familiar mental images that suggest Heaven is a real place with qualities and attributes we will recognize. Why would Paul call our future home by these names if it doesn't in some way resemble a garden, a country, and a city?

, →>>> • <<<<- ‹

The Bible records the eyewitness testimony of men who went into the unseen realm. Their words show us that Heaven is not wispy, ethereal, or otherworldly. It has tangibility and substance. It is a real place with real people who do real things. These writings further reveal that earth is patterned after Heaven. Therefore, we get some idea of what the life to come is like by looking at objects and aspects of life on earth. We can expect our future home to be recognizable and familiar.

I'll address all these points in more detail in upcoming chapters. Before that, however, we need a clear understanding of what happens to us when we die.

WHAT HAPPENS WHEN WE DIE?

*L*ots of people believe that we won't know each other in Heaven or remember our past lives and relationships on earth, all of which makes our future home sound very unappealing. Actually, such ideas are contrary to what the Bible teaches. These misconceptions have developed in part because we lack understanding of what happens when we die.

THE HUMAN MAKEUP

To appreciate what takes place at death, we must first understand the human makeup. All human beings have an outer physical part and an inner immaterial or non-physical part (2 Corinthians 4:16). The outward portion is the body. The inward part consists of spirit and soul (Hebrews 4:12). At death, the inward and the outward portions separate. The outward man returns to dust and the inward man passes into another dimension. We're very familiar with committing bodies to the ground because we've all been to funerals and graveside services. It's the fate of the inward man that is vague.

When Jesus was on earth, He made reference to two men

who died at about the same time. Through His words, He gives a glimpse of the human condition in the unseen dimension.

"There was a rich man who was dressed in purple and fine linen and lived in luxury every day. At his gate was laid a beggar named Lazarus, covered with sores and longing to eat what fell from the rich man's table. Even the dogs came and licked his sores.

The time came when the beggar died and the angels carried him to Abraham's side. [Abraham's side was another name for the home of the righteous dead.] *The rich man also died and was buried. In hell, where he was in torment, he looked up and saw Abraham far away, with Lazarus by his side. So he called to him, 'Father Abraham, have pity on me and send Lazarus to dip the tip of his finger in water and cool my tongue, because I am in agony in this fire.'*

But Abraham replied, 'Son, remember that in your lifetime you received your good things, while Lazarus received bad things, but now he is comforted here and you are in agony. And besides all this, between us and you a great chasm has been fixed, so that those who want to go from here to you cannot, nor can anyone cross over from there to us.' He answered, 'Then I beg you, father, send Lazarus to my father's house, for I have five brothers. Let him warn them, so that they will not also come to this place of torment.'

Abraham replied, 'They have Moses and the Prophets; let them listen to them.' 'No, father Abraham,' he said, 'but if someone from the dead goes to them, they will repent.' He said to him, 'If they do not listen to

Moses and the Prophets, they will not be convinced even if someone rises from the dead'" (Luke 16:19-31, NIV).

Notice that after Lazarus and the rich man were separated from their bodies, they still looked like themselves. They recognized each other and those who had died before them. Both men were fully awake and aware. Each had thoughts, feelings, and recollections of the life and people they left behind. The wealthy gentleman was unhappy about his situation. The beggar was comforted (see note 3). This incident reveals that men and women don't cease to exist when they die. Neither is there a sleep state or state of unconsciousness after death. And not only do human beings live on after they leave their bodies, there is continuation of identity. They're the same people with the same life histories, relationships, and memories.

You may have heard that at death the soul goes to Heaven, giving the impression that only a portion of our being enters the unseen realm. Yet according to the Lord Jesus, the unseen dimension is populated with people who, although separated from their physical bodies, are fully intact. The idea that only our soul goes to Heaven comes from a misunderstanding of what the soul is. The term is most often used in the Scripture to refer to our mental and emotional faculties (Psalm 42:4-6; Psalm 116:7). Based on what Jesus revealed in His account of Lazarus and the rich man, when human beings leave their bodies at death, they take their minds and emotions (their souls) with them.

Moses and Elijah

We get further insight into what happens after death by looking at another instance where people on earth saw a glimpse of the invisible dimension. Not long before Jesus went to the Cross, He took three of His followers (Peter, James, and John) into the mountains. Suddenly, Moses and Elijah, the renowned prophets of Israel, stepped out of the unseen realm. The disciples saw both men and heard them talking with the Lord about His upcoming crucifixion.

> *"About eight days later Jesus took Peter, James, and John to a mountain to pray. And as he was praying, the appearance of his face changed, and his clothing became dazzling white. Then two men, Moses and Elijah, appeared and began talking with Jesus. They were glorious to see. And they were speaking of how he was about to fulfill God's plan by dying in Jerusalem"* (Luke 9:28-31, NLT).

As I pointed out in the first chapter, Elijah went into the unseen dimension in his physical body without experiencing death. Moses, on the other hand, had been dead—or separated from his physical body—for centuries. Yet he was not a floating, transparent soul. He was visible, recognizable, and able to talk with Jesus and Elijah. Moses and Elijah each reflected the brilliance of the dimension that had been their home for centuries. Although they no longer lived on earth, their discussion with Jesus about upcoming events in Jerusalem shows that they were aware of and interested in what was happening here.

WHAT JOHN SAW

John's description in the Book of Revelation of the people he saw in Heaven is very similar to what Jesus revealed in His account of Lazarus and the rich man. And John's report is consistent with what he, Peter, and James saw when Moses and Elijah spoke to Jesus before the crucifixion. John described twenty-four elders, or persons of authority, sitting on thrones. Even though these men were disembodied (separated from their bodies), they wore crowns and clothing, sat on thrones, fell down, and worshipped God, indicating they have heads, mouths, voices, legs, arms, and hands (Revelation 4:4-10). John witnessed continuity of identity in Heaven. He saw people who had been killed for their faith in Christ, yet they remembered their lives on earth and were concerned about those left behind.

> *"When he opened the fifth seal, I saw under the altar the souls of those who had been slain because of the word of God and the testimony they had maintained. They called out in a loud voice, 'How long, Sovereign Lord, holy and true, until you judge the inhabitants of the earth and avenge our blood?' Then each of them was given a white robe, and they were told to wait a little longer, until the number of their fellow servants and brothers who were to be killed as they had been was completed"* (Revelation 6:9-11, NIV).

The apostle's use of the term *souls* doesn't refer to nebulous dots or some portion of these people. It means them. John wrote his account in Greek and used the word *psuche* for souls. *Psuche* is used elsewhere in the Bible to mean "whole person" (1 Corinthians 15:45) (Strong 2004). In other words, John stated that he saw them in Heaven. Notice that these martyrs remember how they died and know that others on earth will die as they had. John heard them raise their voices in emotional expressions as they asked the Lord to take action and administer justice on behalf of those killed (see note 4).

DEATH RELOCATES PEOPLE

Paul, a man who visited Heaven during his lifetime, referred to death as a departure. While he was in prison facing a possible death sentence, he wrote that he had *"a desire to **depart,** and to be with Christ"* (Philippians 1:23, KJV). Paul didn't die at that time, but several years later—when he was once again imprisoned and approaching his death—he wrote, *"the time of my **departure** is at hand"* (2 Timothy 4:6, KJV). When you depart, you leave one place to go to another. Death doesn't turn us into someone or something else. It relocates us from the visible dimension to the invisible.

You will still be you in Heaven. Part of what makes you *you* is your physical appearance, life experiences, relationships, and memories. If you lose any of those qualities and are no longer recognizable or able to remember your life on earth, then you didn't go to Heaven—someone else did. You will be you—minus the effects of living in a damaged world filled with accidents, disease, debilitating infirmities, and the ravages of old age. Earlier in the chapter, we referenced Jesus' account of Lazarus the beggar. When he separated from his body, Lazarus (the man on the inside) left behind the effects of poverty and hunger and the toll they took on him. He had no more painful sores for dogs to lick.

When you exit your body at death, you'll leave behind the illness or injury that ended your life. If you had a chronic condition or disability that affected the course of your life in some way, it will be gone. Memories wiped out by cognitive impairments and dementia will be restored. Those who die before they are old enough to experience life, accumulate memories, and develop relationships will have those opportunities restored in our future home. I'll expand on these issues in later chapters.

· ->>>> · <<<<- ·

There is continuity of identity in Heaven. Men and women look like themselves and retain their life histories. They're no less real than when they lived on earth. The primary difference is that most of them are separated from their physical bodies. Disembodied people aren't ghostly and transparent. They don't float around. They stand, walk, and talk in a realm that, although invisible to us, has physicality and substance.

Now that we have a better understanding of what happens at death, we're ready to take a look at what life is like in Heaven.

LIFE IN HEAVEN

*H*eaven sounds unattractive because it seems boring: an unending worship service where everyone is dressed in white robes and doing nothing but singing and playing harps. But according to the Bible, that's not what life is like in our future home. God's Word makes it clear that just as personal identity continues, so do certain aspects of life as we know it. Scripture reveals a dimension with food and clothing as well as meaningful work and activities.

FOOD IN HEAVEN

The Lord Jesus Christ Himself stated that people in the unseen realm feast together. He told his followers that as part of their reward for faithful service to Him, *"ye may **eat and drink** at my table in my kingdom"* (Luke 22:30, KJV). He further disclosed *"that many will come from the east and the west, and will **take their places at the feast** with Abraham, Isaac and Jacob in the kingdom of heaven"* (Matthew 8:11, NIV). The phrase *take their places* comes from a word in the Greek language that means "to lean back or recline" (Strong 2004). In that day, people reclined on couches as they ate. They placed their heads toward the table and their feet away from it. Jesus' use of this word indicates a place at a table for a meal.

Jesus wasn't speaking symbolically or metaphorically. He described real activity in a real place. Feasting requires tables and chairs and buildings to house the furniture. Special meals involve various foods and drinks as well as utensils for preparing, serving, and eating. And no banquet is complete without conversation, storytelling, and laughter. Jesus' comments about eating and drinking imply the presence of all these elements in the invisible dimension.

Eating is Enjoyable and Relational

Obviously, people in Heaven don't need to eat to sustain life. But eating is more than functional, more than subsistence. The Lord directed Adam and Eve to eat before they became subject to death through sin. The Garden of Eden was filled with edible produce that appealed to their senses of taste, smell, and sight. Consuming food was supposed to be a source of enjoyment provided by their Creator.

> *"And the Lord God planted all sorts of trees in the garden—**beautiful trees** that produced **delicious fruit**...* [God said] *You may freely eat any fruit in the garden except fruit from the tree of the knowledge of good and evil. If you eat of its fruit, you will surely die"* (Genesis 2:9; Genesis 2:16-17, NLT).

Not only is eating enjoyable, it is relational. The Bible records a number of examples of men and women gathering together to eat in the Lord's presence at His command.

* "[At God's invitation] *Moses, Aaron...and seventy of the*

leaders of Israel went up [Mount Sinai]. *There they saw the God of Israel.* [The unseen realm opened to them.] *Under his feet there seemed to be a pavement of brilliant sapphire, as clear as the heavens.* [And] **they shared a meal together in God's presence**" (Exodus 24:9-11, NLT).

- The Lord instructed His people to bring their sacrifices and offerings to His Tabernacle "[where] **you and your families will feast in the presence of the Lord your God, and you will rejoice**" (Deuteronomy 12:7, NLT).

- He gave these specific directions: If you live far away you can *"sell the tithe portion of your crops and herds and take the money* [to the Tabernacle]. *When you arrive, use the money to buy anything you want—an ox, a sheep, some wine, or beer.* **Then feast there in the presence of the Lord your God and celebrate with your household**" (Deuteronomy 14:25-26, NLT).

There's a common theme in these passages: Almighty God called His people to feast with each other and with Him. It makes sense, then, that we'll continue to dine together in the Lord's presence when we actually live with Him in His home.

CLOTHING IN HEAVEN

The Bible mentions clothing in Heaven. Angels, who make up part of the inhabitants of the unseen realm, are described as being clothed.

"Suddenly [on resurrection morning] *there was a great earthquake, because an angel of the Lord came down from heaven and rolled aside the stone* [blocking the entrance to Jesus' tomb] *and sat on it. His face*

*shone like lightning, and his **clothing** was as white as snow"* (Matthew 28:2-3, NLT).

When Moses and Elijah stepped out of the invisible dimension to speak with Jesus before His crucifixion, it's implied that they wore clothing since Jesus' clothes are mentioned. It's silly to think that the two of them were unclothed while Jesus was fully dressed.

"As the men [Peter, James, and John] *watched, Jesus' appearance changed so that his face shone like the sun, and his **clothing** became dazzling white. Suddenly, Moses and Elijah appeared and began talking with Jesus"* (Matthew 17:2-3, NLT).

During his time in Heaven, the apostle John saw multitudes of people wearing white garments.

- He recorded that *"twenty-four elders sat on* [thrones and] *they were all **clothed in white**"* and wrote that those *"who had been martyred...*[were given] ***a white robe.***" He reported seeing *"a vast crowd...**clothed in white**"* (Revelation 4:4; Revelation 6:9-11; Revelation 7:9, NLT).

- John observed people celebrating with Jesus. They too were clothed in *"the **finest white linen**,"* and he watched armies *"dressed in **pure white linen**"* come out of Heaven with the Lord (Revelation 19:8; Revelation 19:14, NLT).

Are White Robes Our Eternal Destiny?

It's hard to read John's description of heavenly attire without thinking of choir robes or burial shrouds. But when we understand what these garments represent, we can be excited about them. They symbolize the sinlessness that the wearers possess through Jesus. One of the twenty-four elders who sits near the throne of God said as much when he told John: *"These are they which came out of great tribulation, and have washed their robes, and made them white in the blood of the Lamb"* (Revelation 7:14, KJV). People in Heaven are so completely cleansed from sin because of the shed blood of Jesus Christ that they can stand before the throne of God with no trace of their past transgressions.

Although John didn't mention other types of clothing, the Bible gives strong indication that white outfits aren't the only clothes we'll wear. You see, John's account of Heaven is not a description of everyday life and apparel in our future home. The apostle was taken into Heaven to observe and record a vision of events immediately preceding the Second Coming of Jesus. John witnessed unique activities connected with the Lord's return. It's therefore highly likely that the white garments John saw are special vestments for special occasions and that we will wear different clothing at other times.

Jesus suggested as much in a parable He told. He spoke of a wealthy man's son who took his inheritance, left home, and wasted his fortune on riotous, sinful activities. The young man—when he was reduced to living in a pigpen—had a change of heart and decided to go home. The wayward son's loving father warmly welcomed him with new clothes and a grand party.

> *"But the father said to his servants, Bring forth the **best robe**, and put it on him; and put a ring on his hand, and shoes on his feet: And bring hither the fatted calf, and kill it; and let us eat, and be merry"* (Luke 15:22-23, KJV).

47

Jesus related the story to illustrate how Heaven responds when a sinner comes back to God. In doing so, our Lord gave us some insight into life in Heaven. Notice one point for now. The son was given a robe to wear at the celebration about to take place. The people Jesus first spoke the parable to would have been familiar with this type of robe. It was a vestment used in their culture only on certain days, such as birthdays or festival days. When the party was over and the son returned to everyday life in his father's home, he would have put on other, more appropriate dress. Surely the parable doesn't have more benefits than the reality of Heaven itself. If there are special clothes for special occasions once we're back in our Father's house, there are most likely outfits for work and play. I'll say more about clothing in the life to come in a later chapter.

WORK IN HEAVEN

People don't look forward to Heaven because they can't imagine what we'll do for eternity. Plus, it's hard to envision doing something we actually enjoy because it seems sacrilegious. Nonetheless, based on Paul's assertion that to *"die is gain,"* we can presume that whatever we do in the life ahead, it will be more satisfying and fulfilling than anything we've ever known.

Before discussing activities in Heaven, I need to address a few basic facts about what we have been created to do. Almighty God designed us to glorify Him through worship and service. This is our created purpose.

"Fear God—know that He is, revere and worship Him—and keep His commandments; for this is the whole of man [the full original purpose of his creation, the object of God's providence, the root of char-

acter, the foundation of all happiness...]" (Ecclesiastes 12:13, AMP).

I suspect that what I just said is less than comforting because it sounds like I'm reinforcing the concept of an endless church service in Heaven. However, this idea stems from our misconceptions about what it means to worship and serve the Lord. We think worshipping God is an activity done in Sunday church. But worship involves much more than singing a few songs during church service. Let's revisit Eden for greater insight into this issue.

Work in Eden

The first time the idea of work appears in the Scripture is in connection with the Garden of Eden. *"And the Lord God took the man, and put him into the garden of Eden to **dress** it and to **keep** it"* (Genesis 2:15, KJV). The word *dress* in the original Hebrew language is one of several words for work. The Hebrew word that is translated *keep* means "to watch or care for" (Strong 2004). You may wonder why man had to work in Paradise and why the Garden needed someone to take care of it. The Lord God created the plant kingdom in a state of maturity so that its harvest was available when man came on the scene. Because the Garden produced spontaneously, it needed maintenance in order to prevent profuse growth. That was the job God assigned to Adam.

This same word translated *dress* is used elsewhere in Scripture to mean "worship and serve" (Exodus 3:12; Joshua 24:15) (Strong 2004). As I said earlier, we've mistakenly relegated both actions to church-related enterprises. Since service to God is man's created purpose, it must be something that everyone in every generation can do, no matter what their lot is in life.

Adam and Eve were able to serve and glorify Almighty God in an outdoor garden before church buildings, hymn books, and preachers existed.

- Paul told slaves in the Roman Empire to perform their menial tasks for the glory of God. *"Slaves, your job is to obey your human masters, not with the idea of catching their eye or currying favour, but as a sincere expression of your devotion to the Lord.* ***Whatever your task is, put your whole heart and soul into it, as into work done for the Lord and not merely for men***—*knowing that your real reward will come from him. You are actually slaves of the Lord Christ Jesus"* (Colossians 3:22-24, J. B. Phillips).

- Paul wrote to Christians in Greece, *"So then, whether you eat or drink, or* ***whatever you may do, do all for the honor and glory of God"*** (1 Corinthians 10:31, AMP).

Everything we do is supposed to be an expression of reverence and honor to the Lord. Each thought, word, and deed is meant to be a demonstration of our trust in, love for, and dependence on Him. And all activities—whether we're singing a song, drinking a glass of milk, or planting a tree—are intended to be a source of joyful fulfillment for us.

No More Toil

Human beings have a God-given desire for meaningful, satisfying activity. That's not wrong. It's part of who we are as God's creation. Work was never meant to be the difficult drudgery it often is in this life. According to God's Word, toilsome labor is a consequence of Adam's sin.

"[God said]...*'Cursed is the ground because of you*

[Adam]*; through **painful toil** you will eat of it all the days of your life. It will produce thorns and thistles for you, and you will eat the plants of the field. By the sweat of your brow you will eat your food until you return to the ground, since from it you were taken'"* (Genesis 3:17-19, NIV).

All this is going to change in the life ahead. Work will finally become what it was meant to be from the beginning—a gratifying endeavor that brings glory to the Lord and builds up our fellow man. We'll fulfill our created purpose because everything we do will be an act of service or worship to Almighty God. Yes, there will be times of corporate worship in Heaven. John witnessed several. But the Bible reveals that there will be a lot of other action in our future home—both work and play. What kinds of things will we do? I'll give specifics in later chapters, but here's a hint: many of the activities we now enjoy will continue in the life to come.

KNOWLEDGE AND TIME IN HEAVEN

I've had more than one person tell me that we'll instantly know everything in Heaven. I've heard others say that there will be no time in eternity. Both statements are inaccurate and add to the lack of excitement about what lies ahead. If we have complete knowledge in a realm with no passage of time, then that means there will be no changes or challenges. Granted, challenges and changes can be troublesome in this life, but lack of these elements makes Heaven seem so monotonous.

Instant Knowledge

The idea that we'll immediately possess all knowledge comes from misunderstanding a passage written by the apostle Paul:

51

*"Now we see but a poor reflection as in a mirror; then we shall see face to face. Now I **know** in part; then I shall **know** fully, even as I am fully **known**"* (1 Corinthians 13:12, NIV).

Paul did not say we'll know everything. He was expressing the idea that in Heaven, we'll see things more clearly and, therefore, more accurately. If the apostle wanted to say that we'll possess all knowledge, he would have used different wording. Instead, he used variations of the same Greek word three times (*know, know,* and *known*). It means "to come to know, recognize, understand, or to understand completely" (Vine 1984).

Paul's example of a poor reflection in a mirror makes his meaning plain. The city of Corinth, home of the Christians to whom he wrote, was known for its polished bronze mirrors. His readers were well familiar with the fact that these all-metal mirrors didn't produce a clear reflection and distorted the images. Since their culture equated seeing with knowing, they got his point. None of us see clearly. Due to the effect of sin on humanity, we all have misperceptions about reality. But in Heaven, those misperceptions will vanish and we will know accurately.

While John was in Heaven, he heard men and women ask God when He is going to carry out justice in the earth. They were told it would be a while longer. These people asked for and were given information they didn't have even though they were in Heaven. In other words, they learned something new.

" 'How long, Sovereign Lord, holy and true, until you judge the inhabitants of the earth and avenge our blood'...they were told to wait a little longer, until the number of their fellow servants and brothers who

were to be killed as they had been was completed"
(Revelation 6:10-11, NIV).

We'll never know everything—ever. Only God knows everything. Omniscience or All-Knowingness is a characteristic of Deity. We are and always will be created, finite beings with definable limits—even in Heaven. God knows us fully, without any misconceptions, but we'll never exhaust all there is to know from and about Almighty God. He is Infinite.

No More Time

The idea that there's no time in Heaven is very common, but this is also contrary to what the Bible discloses. John made numerous references to the passage of time in the unseen realm.

- I cited the verses above where he reported that the martyrs in Heaven who long for justice on the earth were told to *"wait **a little longer"*** (Revelation 6:11, NIV).

- When John was in the invisible dimension, he saw men and women *"standing in front of the throne of God, serving him **day and night** in his Temple"* (Revelation 7:15, NLT).

- The apostle described *"silence throughout heaven for about **half an hour"*** (Revelation 8:1, NLT).

- He quoted Jesus as referring to *"the tree of life in the paradise of God...bearing twelve crops of fruit, with a fresh crop **each month"*** (Revelation 2:7, Revelation 22:2, NLT).

John also reported that he heard an angel proclaim *"that there should be time no longer"* (Revelation 10:6, KJV). Some cite his words as proof that there will be no time in Heaven. But that's not the idea in the original language. According to *The Expanded Vine's Dictionary of New Testament Words* (1984), the Greek word translated *time* means "delay." The angel whom John heard utter these words declared that there's no time left before God's judgment is carried out and His plan of redemption is fulfilled.

> *"There shall be **no more delay**! In the days which shall soon be announced by the trumpet-blast of the seventh angel the mysterious purpose of God shall be completed, as he assured his servants the prophets"* (Revelation 10:6-7, J. B. Phillips).

No More Process

Many also believe that everything will always stay the same in Heaven. But that's not so. There will be process in eternity. *Webster's New Students Dictionary* (1969) defines *process* as "a series of actions, operations, or changes [leading] to an end." Time and process are linked to each other because time passes when a sequence of actions occurs. John saw many sequential events in Heaven (e.g., seven seals opened, one following another; seven trumpets blown, each following the other; seven bowls poured out, one after another). He heard people singing. Songs have time or tempo with a beginning, middle, and ending, and they progress sequentially. In eternity, we'll live in time without the pressure that time is running out.

Consider what Paul said about the life to come. He stated that throughout all eternity, the Lord God will increasingly reveal more and more of what His grace has provided for those who have accepted His salvation. This is unending process and ongoing revelation.

"And [God] *raised us up with Him* [Jesus] *and seated us with Him in the heavenly places in Christ Jesus, so that **in the ages to come** He might show the surpassing riches of His grace in kindness toward us in Christ Jesus"* (Ephesians 2:6-7, NASB).

› ‑››› · ‹‹‹‑ ‹

We'll examine life in Heaven in greater detail in the second half of this book. But be encouraged that Heaven is a real place with real people who do real things, many of the same things we do on earth. The life to come won't be foreign or freaky to us. It will feel like home.

Before we say more about the particulars of life in our forever home, we need to consider what people are like in Heaven.

WHAT WILL WE BE LIKE IN HEAVEN?

We have many inaccurate ideas about the life to come. We've been told that relationships with family and friends will end and we'll want no one but God. Some say we lose our individuality and become part of a big communal group that does nothing but worship the Lord. No wonder we don't look forward to Heaven. Happily, the Bible reveals that we'll still be individual people with distinct personalities, and our relationships with friends and loved ones will continue.

THE BIG PICTURE

Misconceptions about life after death come from not understanding God's overall purpose for man. When we consider Heaven in terms of the big picture, it makes no sense that we'll no longer be recognizable or different from each other. Space doesn't permit a detailed study of the Lord's plan, but here are a few brief highlights:

- In eternity past, the Lord God conceived a plan to create men and women in His image and make them His family. However, the first man (Adam) chose independence from the Lord through sin. His disobedience affected the whole race in him and fundamentally altered human nature. Since that time, all human beings are born into a damaged race with a nature contrary to God, which they express through sinful actions (Romans 3:23; Romans 5:19; Ephesians 2:1-3).

• The Lord devised a way to save mankind from this condition and regain His family. Because of the death, burial, and resurrection of Jesus Christ, God is able to redeem or deliver sinful people from the guilt, power, and damage of sin and transform them into holy, righteous sons and daughters. Jesus is our Redeemer.

• *"For consider what he has done—before the foundation of the world he chose us to be, in Christ, his children, holy and blameless in his sight. He planned, in his love, that we should be adopted as his own children through Jesus Christ...It is through him, at the cost of his own blood, that we are redeemed"* (Ephesians 1:4-7, J. B. Phillips).

At the Cross, Jesus Christ paid the price for sin so it can be removed. When we accept His sacrifice, our sins are washed away and we receive eternal life. *"For God so loved the world that he gave his one and only Son, that whoever believes in him shall not perish but have eternal life"* (John 3:16, NIV). This eternal life is more than length of life. All human beings have eternal life in the sense that no one ceases to exist when their physical body dies. The only question is, where will we live— forever with God in His home or forever separated from Him?

The eternal life that Almighty God gives to those who believe in Jesus is a *type* of life. When we acknowledge Jesus as Savior and Lord, God imparts something of Himself to us. His own uncreated, eternal life floods our innermost being (our spirit) and we're literally born of Him (1 John 5:1; John 1:12). This new birth begins a process of transformation that ultimately restores us to what the Lord always intended—sons and daughters who are blameless and holy in every part of our makeup. This metamorphosis starts when we're born again, progresses during our lifetime, and is completed in the life to come. The Bible refers to the present inhabitants of Heaven as *"the righteous [the redeemed in heaven] who have been made perfect"* (Hebrews 12:23, AMP).

Almighty God's goal in redemption is to free our entire being from sin and its effects, not turn us into someone or something else. His aim is to perfect us, not erase or replace us. In the life to come, we'll be everything the Lord always wanted us to be. That's God's plan.

You are more than your physical appearance. What makes you *you* is your life history, relationships, and experiences—it's your personality and talents, abilities and interests, likes and dislikes. Admittedly, these various traits have been tainted by sin, but they will be cleansed in Heaven. You'll become the *you* you were meant to be. This doesn't negate the fact that we can and should grow in Christ-like character and holiness in this life. Just know that the process will not be fully complete until we get to Heaven.

God Made Us Different

We won't all be the same in Heaven because we aren't now. Uniqueness and individuality are part of God's design for His family. All the various people groups on earth were resident in Adam when the Lord fashioned him: *"From one ancestor [Adam] he [God] has created every race of men to live over the face of the whole earth"* (Acts 17:26, J. B. Phillips). The first two humans, Adam and Eve, were different from each other. He was male. She was female. He was bigger and stronger. She was beautiful.

Perhaps you're thinking, "Doesn't the Bible say we'll no longer be male or female in Heaven? After all, Galatians 3:28 says, *'There is neither Jew nor Greek, slave nor free, male nor female, for you are all one in Christ Jesus'*" (NIV). This passage doesn't mean we lose our gender identity. Based on the context, it's clear that this statement refers to the equality of men and women in Christ. We'll continue to be equally valuable to God in our eternal home, but we'll still be different from one another.

The apostle John confirmed that we retain our individuality and uniqueness in Heaven. Even though he saw a huge crowd of people—more than he could number—he was able to recognize that the multitude was made up of distinct ethnic groups. This wouldn't have been possible unless these men and women retained traits specific to their nationalities.

> *"After this I saw a vast crowd, too great to count,* **from every nation and tribe and people and language**, *standing in front of the throne and before the Lamb"* (Revelation 7:9, NLT).

NOTHING BUT GOD

Maybe you've heard it said that in Heaven we'll want nothing and no one but the Lord. Although this sounds super spiritual, such thinking is based on a faulty premise—that finding joy in or longing for anything or anyone other than God is somehow wrong. Of course, the supreme and greatest joy of Heaven is seeing the Lord face-to-face and knowing Him in a way that we do not now. Imagine the delight of beholding the One who created us for Himself, the One who loves us and has redeemed us for a wonderful purpose and future. Still, the fact that the Lord God is the primary delight of Heaven doesn't mean there aren't other joys.

- Because relationships continue into the next life, we'll still have affection for those we knew and loved on earth. Just think of the joy you'll feel when you're reunited with a loved one you haven't seen in years because they went to Heaven before you.

- And since we retain our God-given uniqueness in eternity, we'll have many of the same interests and passions we had on earth. Imagine the pleasure you'll derive from pursuing them without the roadblocks this life often brings our way.

Interests and emotions won't be obliterated in the life to come. Instead, they'll be purified and the flaws and effects of sin removed forever. The struggle with desires that sometimes drive us to act in ungodly ways will be gone. Our yearnings and feelings will function as they were meant to, in God-glorifying expressions. We'll long to please the Lord in every part of our being and be completely able to do so.

The Source of All Good Things

It's not wrong to find pleasure in something other than God. The Bible says He is the source of all good things and instructs us to be grateful for and enjoy His many gifts. This won't change in Heaven.

"Every good thing given and every perfect gift is from above, coming down from the Father of lights,

with whom there is no variation or shifting shadow" (James 1:17, NASB).

"God...richly and ceaselessly provides us with everything for [our] enjoyment" (1 Timothy 6:17, AMP).

"For everything God created is good, and nothing is to be rejected if it is received with thanksgiving, because it is consecrated by the word of God and prayer" (1 Timothy 4:4-5, NIV).

When we desire and delight in what the Lord has created, we magnify Him. Gratefully enjoying vegetables grown in your garden glorifies the ultimate source of the provision, the Lord God. Expressing thankfulness for your house and car honors the Lord because He created the raw materials that were used to make them and He gave men the ingenuity to produce them. Yes, it's presently possible to put people and things above God since we aren't entirely free from sin's influence yet. That won't be the case in Heaven.

No One But God?

The Lord created us to desire a relationship with Himself above everything. At the same time, He also made us to need other people. After God formed Adam, the two of them walked and talked together. Yet the Lord referred to Adam as being alone and said it wasn't good—not in a moral sense, but because He never intended to make just one human. Almighty God created Adam (and man in Adam) with a desire for companionship with others like himself.

"Now the Lord God said, It is not good [sufficient, satisfactory] that the man should be alone; I will make

him a helper meet (suitable, adapted, completing) for him" (Genesis 2:18, AMP).

When Adam first saw Eve, his response was, *"At last!"* (Genesis 2:23, NLT). God didn't rebuke Adam for his excitement over someone besides Him. In fact, the Lord blessed the two of them and established the committed relationship we call marriage (Genesis 2:23-25).

Finding joy and delight in other people isn't sinful. Relationship with others doesn't necessarily distract us from the Lord. In fact, a good friend—someone in whom you see God and who helps you demonstrate Christ-like character more effectively—can make you a better person.

- Jesus spent a lot of time with people when He was on earth. He even had an inner circle—John, Peter, and James. Certainly, these friendships didn't distract Jesus from His Father.

- Paul wrote of his affection for the Christians in the city of Philippi and his desire to be with them: *"God can testify how I long for all of you with the affection of Christ Jesus"* (Philippians 1:8, NIV). Clearly, love for these people didn't diminish his passion for God.

Going to Heaven doesn't negate relationships established on earth. Nothing will change our past history—the fact that we were part of a family or that we had a close friendship with another person. Paul knew that part of the reward awaiting him in Heaven was ongoing relationships with those he'd won to faith in Christ.

"After all, what gives us hope and joy, and what is our

proud reward and crown? It is you! Yes, you will bring us much joy as we stand together before our Lord Jesus...For you are our pride and joy" (1 Thessalonians 2:19-20, NLT).

THE LAW OF LOVE

Jesus said that the entirety of God's Law is summed up in two commands: love God and love your neighbor (Matthew 22:37-40). Adam was under this Law of Love in the Garden of Eden: *"For the original command, as you know, is that we should love one another"* (1 John 3:11, J. B. Phillips). This eternal command to love won't cease to exist in Heaven. And because we'll be fully perfected, we'll be able to love the Lord and each other perfectly.

Human interactions will come out of righteousness or rightness. There will be no pride or insecurities and no need to exalt self and put others down. Hidden agendas, betrayals, pretenses, sharp tongues, outbursts of rage, and insincerity won't exist. It's hard to imagine the perfect harmony and fulfillment that will exist in relationships with family and friends in our future home. Relationships with those we already know will deepen as we make new connections with people we've not yet met—like ancestors, men and women mentioned in the Bible, and people from other countries!

God is the Father of everyone in Heaven, and all the human residents are His sons and daughters. This means we'll have kinship with those who were blood relatives on earth, but we'll also have it with friends. We'll be one big, happy, healthy family and finally treat each other as the Lord desires. Heaven is the culmination of Almighty God's plan to redeem and restore everything that has been damaged by sin, including relationships.

I Don't Want to See That Person in Heaven!

Possibly, there's someone you don't want to see in Heaven. You don't necessarily want them to go to Hell. You just don't care to run into them in eternity. Several people have admitted to me that they dread the thought of coming face-to-face with a particular person in the life to come. They include:

- A woman who had an abortion and dreads seeing the child because she feels guilty about what she did.

- A lady who had a falling out with a friend and the conflict wasn't resolved before the former friend died.

- A man who was directly responsible for his own mother's death before he committed his life to Jesus Christ.

- A daughter whose father caused great emotional and physical damage to her through abuse—although he repented and received God's saving grace on his deathbed, she wants him as far away from her as possible.

The Bible gives us good news. These kinds of issues will be resolved and the hurts and harm caused by relational challenges will be healed once we're all perfected. Your loved one who inflicted pain on you will be transformed and you will be completely free from the damage done. If you harmed someone in this life, there will be forgiveness and restoration.

Remember the parable of the prodigal son referenced in the previous chapter? Jesus told the story to illustrate how Heaven responds when a lost son or daughter comes back to God. He shared an interesting detail that relates to the restoration of damaged relationships. As you recall, the young man took his inheritance, abandoned the family, and wasted all the money his father gave him on booze and prostitutes. When the son finally returned home, his father welcomed him. Although the boy greatly wronged his father, there was no mention of it—no "How could you have done this to me" lecture from the older man. Instead, dad hugged and kissed him and threw a party. He knew his son was truly sorry and all was forgiven and forgotten.

> *"So he returned home to his father. And while he was still a long distance away, his father saw him coming. Filled with love and compassion, he ran to his son, embraced him, and kissed him. His son said to him, 'Father, I have sinned against both heaven and you, and I am no longer worthy of being called your son.' But his father said to the servants, 'Quick! ...We must celebrate with a feast, for this son of mine was dead and has now returned to life. He was lost, but now he is found.' So the party began"* (Luke 15:20-24, NLT).

I can't explain how every relational difficulty will be resolved. But God's Word has persuaded me that what's ahead is gain, not loss—better, not worse. Therefore, we can rest in the certainty that, however it works, everything will be made right and we don't have to dread any aspect of Heaven.

What About Loved Ones in Hell?

What about someone you hoped to see in Heaven, but they didn't make it? How can you be happy in the life to come if a friend or loved one is in Hell? The answer to this question could fill an entire book; but, hopefully, the following thoughts will be helpful.

All human beings are guilty of sin before a holy God. That's hard for us to imagine because most of us consider ourselves and our friends and loved ones to be good people. However, the standard for how good we must be to enter Heaven is God Himself, and none of us measure up to the mark. *"For all have sinned; all fall short of God's glorious standard"* (Romans 3:23, NLT).

Jesus died on the Cross to pay the price for our sin so it can be removed and we can be declared not guilty. His sacrifice at Calvary gives us the righteousness necessary to enter God's kingdom. Jesus is the door to Heaven. Our Savior said, *"I am the Way and the Truth and the Life; no one comes to the Father except by (through) Me"* (John 14:6, AMP). Entrance to Heaven is based on God's grace given to us through Jesus when we believe on Him and His saving work—not on how good we are.

God loves humankind and does all He can to draw men and women back to Him through Christ. He's not willing that any miss the purpose for which He created us—sonship and relationship with Him in His eternal home. *"God...wants everyone to turn from sin and no one to be lost"* (2 Peter 3:9, CEV). But Almighty God doesn't force anyone to acknowledge Jesus or serve Him. All who choose to live separated from Him in this life will continue to do so in the life to come. That's what Hell is—a complete separation from God with all the ensuing consequences. There's no one in Hell who has not chosen to be there. The Lord sends no one to Hell. Men and women choose it (see note 5).

When John was taken to Heaven and given a vision of the culmination of God's plan of redemption, he saw the final judgment of those who throughout history have refused the Lord. The record books were opened to show definitively that

God is right to forever confine to Hell those who've elected to be His enemies (Revelation 20:11-15). In connection with these events, John witnessed all the inhabitants of Heaven—angels along with men and women—praising God for His righteousness and justice (Revelation 15:3; Revelation 16:7; Revelation 19:2). The clear implication is that we too will participate in praising God for administering justice.

The Bible states that there are no tears of sorrow in Heaven (Revelation 21:4). This means that no one in the unseen realm cries over people in Hell. Although that's hard to envision right now, once we're in Heaven, our perspective will change. In the life to come, we will see things more clearly and, therefore, more accurately (1 Corinthians 13:12). We'll recognize that all human beings, including our loved ones, had enough light given to them to respond to the Lord, but said no. We'll realize that it's right and just that all who have rejected God's gift of salvation through the Cross of Christ be confined to a place of everlasting separation.

' ⇢⟩⟩⟩ ' ⟨⟨⟨⟨⟵ '

Almighty God's intention in salvation isn't to replace us or turn us into someone else. His aim is to transform us by His power and restore us to what He always intended: sons and daughters free from every trace and effect of sin, able to perfectly love Him and love His people. We will realize this purpose in the life to come.

Later in the book, I'll go into more detail about how our individuality and uniqueness is going to be expressed in our future home. But first I need to address a much-misunderstood subject that makes many people less than eager to go to Heaven—marriage in Heaven.

MARRIAGE IN HEAVEN

I've had more than one happily married older couple tell me how sad they are that they won't know each other in Heaven and their life together will be over. When I protest, they forlornly remind me that Jesus said there's no more marriage in the life ahead. Not only is this common belief incorrect, it greatly enhances Heaven's supposed unattractiveness. The Lord did indeed make the statement, *"For in the resurrection they neither marry, nor are given in marriage, but are as the angels of God in heaven"* (Matthew 22:30, KJV). But when we examine His words in their original setting, it's obvious that He wasn't telling married people that their spouse will no longer be their spouse. Let's take a closer look and sort this out.

ESCAPING THE TRAP

The religious leaders of the day, the Pharisees and the Sadducees, didn't accept Jesus—either His Person or His teachings. In fact, they held strategy sessions to discuss how to discredit Him in front of His followers. They had one of those meetings just prior to an encounter with Jesus that led Him to make the misunderstood statement about marriage in Heaven.

The Pharisees were the first to confront Jesus. They asked Him if it was right for a follower of God to pay taxes to the Roman government. Jesus was aware of their wicked intentions and answered them in a manner that amazed onlookers.

> *"'Here, show me the Roman coin used for the tax.' When they handed him the coin, he asked, 'Whose picture and title are stamped on it?' 'Caesar's,' they replied. 'Well, then,' he said, 'give to Caesar what belongs to him. But everything that belongs to God must be given to God.' His reply amazed them, and they went away'"* (Matthew 22:19-22, NLT).

Then the Sadducees posed a question about marriage. Their religious law stated that if a man died without having children, his brother had to marry the widow, father a child, and raise the child as his brother's heir. These leaders presented such a case to Jesus but said that the man who married his brother's widow also died childless. So the next brother wed the woman, but he too passed away. They took their example through seven brothers, all of whom married the woman and departed this life without fathering an heir. Eventually, she also died. The Sadducees asked Jesus, *"So tell us, whose wife will she be **in the resurrection**?"* (Matthew 22:28, NLT).

I've highlighted the last part of their question because it is the key to understanding Jesus' answer. The term *resurrection* refers to a commonly held belief in that day that the dead will one day be reunited with their bodies raised from the grave. However, the men who asked this question didn't believe in the survival of human beings beyond death or in a coming resurrection. So they weren't interested in gaining information about marriage in the life to come. Instead, these religious leaders hoped to stump Jesus with their example and thereby discredit him. The Lord recognized their true intent and answered them accordingly.

Jesus began by rebuking these men for not knowing their own scriptures. He quoted a passage from the Old Testament where the Lord God called Himself the God of Abraham, Isaac, and Jacob—three well-known and long-dead ancestors of the Sadducees (Exodus 3:6). Jesus then referred to Almighty God as the God of the living and not the dead, indicating that Abraham, Isaac, and Jacob live on and that God, by His power, will one day raise their bodies from the dust. As part of His answer, Jesus made the statement that has led many to believe their relationship with their spouse will come to an end in Heaven.

> *"You are in error because you do not know the Scriptures or the power of God. At the resurrection people will neither marry nor be given in marriage; they will be like the angels in heaven. But about the resurrection of the dead—have you not read what God said to you, 'I am the God of Abraham, the God of Isaac, and the God of Jacob'? He is not the God of the dead but of the living"* (Matthew 22:29-32, NIV).

We cannot use Jesus' words to make definitive statements about husbands and wives in the unseen realm. In the first place, His purpose was not to address the nature of the relationships between married people in Heaven. Jesus was avoiding the trap the Sadducees set when they asked Him to explain something they didn't actually believe in. In the second place, there is much in our Lord's comment about marriage, angels, and the resurrection that no one understands at this point.

We can't let what we don't know undermine what we do know. The Bible is clear that both identity and relationships continue after death. If your mate was your closest companion on earth, that closeness will continue. Granted, God's Word doesn't give specific details about how those who were married on earth will interact with each other. But just know that you won't lose your beloved spouse in the life to come. Heaven is gain, not loss.

NO MARRIAGE IN HEAVEN?

What about those individuals who long to marry but never do or those who are unhappily married? Does Heaven hold any hope for them? Yes! John reported that when he visited the Lord's home, he saw a marriage and a marriage supper—the marriage of the Lamb (Jesus) and His bride (believers in Him).

> *"Then I heard something like the voice of a great multitude and like the sound of many waters and like the sound of mighty peals of thunder, saying, 'Hallelujah! For the Lord our God, the Almighty, reigns. Let us rejoice and be glad and give the glory to Him, for the marriage of the Lamb has come and His bride has made herself ready'"* (Revelation 19:6-7, NASB).

> *"Then he said to me, 'Write, "Blessed are those who are invited to the marriage supper of the Lamb."' And he said to me, 'These are true words of God'"* (Revelation 19:9, NASB).

I realize that John's words may not thrill you because what he witnessed isn't what most of us envision when we think of marriage. Our picture of marriage has been formed primarily by Hollywood—a big, beautiful wedding with a romantic, unending honeymoon. Even the best marriages aren't like what we see in the movies. Real marriage involves two flawed people who come together and attempt to live in harmony as they face the challenges and difficulties of life in a world damaged by sin. Many people end up with something very different than what they were expecting when they walked down the aisle. To appreciate the ceremony and celebration John observed and its impact on our future, we must remember the overall plan of God. Stay with me as I explain.

Union with Christ

Almighty God instituted marriage in the earliest days of human history when He brought Adam and Eve together: *"and the two* [were] *united into one"* (Genesis 2:24, NLT). Marriage serves several practical purposes in this life. It provides companionship with commitment along with a stable structure for establishing a family and producing and rearing children. The imagery of uniting a man and woman together in marriage also illustrates an important aspect of our relationship with Christ—we are united to Him. The apostle Paul wrote:

> *"As the Scriptures say, 'A man leaves his father and mother and is joined to his wife, and the two are united into one.' This is a great mystery, but **it is an illustration of the way Christ and the church** [be-*lievers in Jesus] ***are one"*** (Ephesians 5:31-32, NLT).

When a person acknowledges Jesus as Lord and Savior, that individual, in his innermost being, becomes a partaker of eternal life, or the life in God Himself. As I pointed out in the previous chapter, this inward infusion of life is the beginning of a process of transformation that will ultimately free us from every trace of sin, corruption, and death. The Bible refers to this organic connection as union with Christ. This union is a source of strength, joy, peace, and power as we walk through this world. It's in the life to come, however, that we will be fully cognizant of our union with the Lord and experience everything it provides.

Complete Fulfillment

Every human being longs to be loved and understood. We all want intimacy—not just physical, but emotional and spiritual. We yearn to be connected and accepted, and we look to have those needs met through marriage. When people talk about searching for their soul mate, they often mean, "I'm looking for the one who can fulfill me in every way." Yet no person can satisfy every need we have because total fulfillment comes only through union with God. Only He can complete us. Experiential knowledge of our oneness with Christ and His love and care for us will surpass even the most successful marriage relationships on earth. In Heaven, we'll finally have what our hearts crave and our longings will be satisfied.

I realize that it's difficult to talk about marriage in the context of relationship with Jesus and life after this life. But if we define marriage as a forever union with total love, acceptance, and fulfillment in a specially prepared home, then all who are in Heaven will be married because we're one with the Lord. Granted, much of this is beyond our comprehension right now. But hopefully, you're beginning to see that what's ahead is gain, not loss, even in the area of marriage.

WHAT IS AHEAD?

For those individuals who were blessed with a happy marriage in this life, their relationship will be enhanced by the realization of union with Christ in Heaven. Will you each have separate homes or will you live together? What if you had two happy marriages on earth? Who will you live with? What if you're not happily married and can't wait to get away from your mate?

What if you divorced your spouse because of adultery or abuse and he or she ends up in Heaven? Do you have to be with them again? Although the Bible doesn't address these issues, it gives enough information to assure us that the life ahead outshines anything we've known. It will be right, and it will be better.

Awareness of our future life helps us live this life more effectively. How many people wed someone they shouldn't have because they believed the lie, "If I don't do it now, I'll miss out"? How many singles are angry at God because He hasn't brought them a life partner? What if they knew the truth—that this life is only a shadow of what's to come? If you never marry in this life, have an unhappy marriage, or end up divorced, you can take comfort in the fact that in Heaven, you will have the love and fulfillment you long for through Jesus. And if your marriage has brought you happiness in this life, the best days with your spouse are still to come.

The Plan Completed

Let's go back to John's statement that he saw the marriage supper of the Lamb. His reference to a marriage supper would have painted a vivid picture in the minds of those who first read the account of his visit to Heaven. You see, although the Bible is a timeless book that speaks to every generation, the authors originally wrote to communicate specific information in terms that the men and women of their particular time period would understand.

In John's day and culture, there were three stages to a wedding. The marriage began when two fathers entered into a legal contract that bound their young boy and girl to each other. When the youngsters reached marriage age and the time came to fulfill the contract, the bridegroom left his father's house and set out for his bride. He brought her back home where the two were wed. The ceremony culminated in a gala celebration—a marriage supper where the groom rejoiced with his bride, his family, and his friends. John's first readers knew it was a joyous event marking the fulfillment of a pledge made many years earlier.

While in Heaven, John witnessed the culmination of the plan of redemption. He saw God and His family finally together, celebrating in His home. Like the wedding suppers familiar to John's original readers, the festivities associated with the realization of God's promise to bring us to live with Him forever will be a joyful, glorious celebration unlike anything we've ever experienced!

› →››› · ‹‹‹← ‹

There's much we don't and can't know about Heaven. No words can describe the awesomeness of being in the presence of Almighty God in His home. What will it be like to see Him face-to-face in all His majesty, glory, and holiness? How will it feel to experience a sense of completion and fulfillment along with ultimate joy and peace? Scripture hints at some of these things.

"You will show me the way of life, granting me the joy of your presence and the pleasures of living with you forever" (Psalm 16:11, NLT).

"But as for me, my contentment is not in wealth but in seeing you and knowing all is well between us. And when I awake in heaven, I will be fully satisfied, for I

will see you face to face" (Psalm 17:15, TLB).

Let's not allow what we don't yet understand about our future home undermine what God's Word plainly reveals. We may not have specific details, but we have enough general information to give us a picture of a wonderful place.

- We know that Heaven resembles earth in many ways. It's not wispy, ethereal, or otherworldly. It's a real place with real people who do real things.

- We know that people interact with each other in loving relationships. They remember those they left behind and look forward to reunion. They engage in meaningful, satisfying work and activities. They enjoy life to the fullest as they interact with the Lord.

- We know that the best is yet to come. We won't lose out. We will gain.

PART TWO:

THE NEW EARTH

7

EARTH IS PART OF THE PLAN

e honest. As awesome as the information we've covered so far sounds, most of us would say we're going to miss earth—not the hardships and sufferings of life, but the beauty and wonders of this world. We really don't want to leave the only home we've known. Thankfully, the Bible gives us amazing news: this planet is included in God's eternal plan.

RESURRECTION OF THE DEAD

Much of the confusion about our future arises out of misinformation regarding the ultimate destiny of our physical bodies. As I pointed out in Chapter 3, when human beings die, they separate from their bodies and pass into another dimension. This isn't God's ultimate purpose for man, though. He never intended for us to live as bodiless spirits in an immaterial dimension. The Lord designed us with physical bodies for life in a material world. When God created Adam, He formed the body first and gave human beings senses to enjoy the sights, sounds, scents, tastes, textures, and tactile sensations of earth (Genesis 2:7). Our bodies are neither unimportant nor expendable.

Separation from the body is a temporary state that will be

rectified through resurrection of the dead. Resurrection of the dead is not a freaky, science-fiction event. It's the reuniting of the inward and outward man, which parted ways at death. As part of His plan of redemption, Almighty God will raise our bodies from the grave, or wake them from sleep, and restore them to life. The Bible refers to death of the body as sleep because it is a temporary condition that will be undone through resurrection (Isaiah 26:19; 1 Thessalonians 4:13-14).

When Jesus returns to earth, all who live in the invisible Heaven will come with Him to be reunited with their bodies. The Lord is going to recover our original DNA and restore and reanimate every molecule. Our bodies will be glorified or transformed by eternal life and made incorruptible and immortal. This means they will be completely and forever free of every trace of sickness, infirmity, and old age. They will never again be subject to disease, disability, or death in any form.

> *"For the trumpet shall sound, and the dead shall be raised incorruptible, and we shall be changed. For this corruptible* [body] *must put on incorruption, and this mortal* [body] *must put on immortality. So when this corruptible* [body] *shall have put on incorruption, and this mortal* [body] *shall have put on immortality, then shall be brought to pass the saying that is written,* **Death is swallowed up in victory***"* (1 Corinthians 15:52-54, KJV).

Some say that we'll get new bodies, meaning a different body. This is incorrect. Your resurrection body is your dead body made alive again. It's part of the continuity in the life to come. You go to Heaven, and through resurrection, you are reunited with your original body. The All-Powerful and All-Knowing God is well able to recover what He needs to reanimate and restore our bodies, whether it was torn apart by wild animals, lost at sea, burned up, or disintegrated into dust. Paul the apostle wrote that when Jesus returns, *"He will take these weak mortal bodies of ours and change them into glorious bodies like his own, using the same mighty power that he will use to conquer everything, everywhere"* (Philippians 3:21, NLT).

Our raised bodies will be like Christ's resurrected body. The body that died on the Cross was restored to life and, following His resurrection, Jesus could be seen and touched. He wasn't ghostly. Not only did Jesus look like Himself, He was able to stand, walk, and talk. He even cooked a meal for His disciples and ate and drank with them on several occasions (Luke 24:39-43; Acts 10:41; John 21:9-13).

The Bible doesn't give every detail about the characteristics of our glorified body. For example, it doesn't say how old we'll be. I've heard respected Bible teachers speculate that we'll be thirty-three, the same age as Jesus when His body was raised from the grave. That may be the case. No matter what, based on God's plan for man, we can reasonably conclude that we will be in the prime of life. And Scripture gives us enough information that we can be certain, not only will the original body be made new, it will be perfectly suited for life in a material world. Resurrection from the dead means the restoration of our physical body, so we can live on earth again! That's our future.

A Home for God's Family

Many wrong ideas about what lies ahead come from not understanding Almighty God's overall purpose for mankind. We must remember the plan. The Lord wants sons and daughters, and the Bible reveals that He designed the earth to be home for

His family.

> *"For thus says the Lord Who created the heavens,*
> *God Himself Who formed the earth and made it, Who*
> *established it and created it not a worthless waste; He*
> *formed it to be inhabited"* (Isaiah 45:18, AMP).

Sadly, Adam chose independence from God through sin and rejected his sonship. As the head of the family and first steward of the planet, his actions had a significant impact on both the human race and the earth itself. Not only were men and women made subject to sin and death, the entire physical creation was infused with the curse of death. Plants and animals began to die. Natural laws and processes set into motion by God at the beginning were corrupted. The result was blight, drought, famine, destructive storms, and earthquakes.

> *"When Adam sinned, sin entered the entire human*
> *race. His sin spread death throughout all the world,*
> *so everything began to grow old and die"* (Romans
> 5:12, TLB).

Earth is no longer a fit home for the Lord's family because it's bound by the effects of man's sin. In connection with Jesus Christ's return and resurrection of the dead, the Lord will reclaim what He lost and undo the damage done to the family home.

> *"The creation waits in eager expectation for the*
> *sons of God to be revealed* [at the resurrection of the
> dead]...*We know that the whole creation has been*
> *groaning as in the pains of childbirth right up to the*
> *present time. Not only so, but we ourselves, who have*
> *the firstfruits of the Spirit* [the new birth], *groan in-*

wardly as we wait eagerly for ... the redemption of our bodies [through resurrection of the dead] *"* (Romans 8:19; Romans 8:22-23, NIV).

"For the creation was subjected to frustration [corruption and death], *not by its own choice, but by the will of the one who subjected it* [Adam], *in hope that creation itself will be **liberated** from its bondage to decay and brought into the glorious freedom of the children of God"* (Romans 8:20-21, NIV).

Liberated comes from a word that means "to make free from the power and punishment of sins, the result of redemption" (Strong 2004). As part of God's unfolding plan of redemption, the material creation will be released from decay and mortality just like our physical bodies.

The Lord God is going to reverse the curse of corruption that entered creation when Adam sinned. He'll remove every trace of decay and make this planet a suitable home for His family once again. No more painful toil to eke a living from the ground. No more thorns or thistles. No more corruption. No more death.

DESTROYED BY FIRE?

Lots of people erroneously believe that earth will one day be destroyed by fire. This idea comes from a misinterpretation of a passage the apostle Peter wrote.

*"But the day of the Lord will come as a thief in the night; in the which the heavens shall **pass away** with a great noise, and the **elements shall melt** with fervent heat, the earth also and the works that are there-*

*in shall be **burned up**...all these things shall be **dissolved**...the heavens being on fire shall be **dissolved**,
and the elements **shall melt** with fervent heat"* (2 Peter 3:10-12, KJV).

Peter isn't picturing earth's destruction. He's describing its
transformation. The apostle revealed that when the Lord returns,
the atoms and molecules that make up the physical world will
be freed from their bondage to corruption and death. Peter's
point is obvious when we know the original meaning of key
Greek words.

• *Pass away* is composed of two Greek words meaning "to
come or go by" (Strong 2004). It's used numerous times in
the New Testament and never signifies "cease to exist." It
carries the idea of passing from one condition or state to
another.

• *Elements* is derived from a Greek word that means "the
most basic components of the physical world (atoms and
molecules)" (Strong 2004).

• *Shall melt* (verse 10) and *dissolve* (verses 11 and 12) are
the same word in the original language, *lou*. It means "to
loose" (Strong 2004). Jesus used this term when he raised
Lazarus from the dead. When His friend came out of the
tomb wrapped in grave clothes, Jesus commanded, *"Loose
him, and let him go"* (John 11:44, KJV).

• The phrase *burned up* is not used in the oldest New
Testament manuscripts. Instead, those early copies use
a word that signifies "found or shown" (Strong 2004).
The idea isn't the destruction of earth, but exposure of
corruption for the purpose of removal. *"And the earth and*

everything in it will be laid bare" (2 Peter 3:10, NIV).

- *Shall melt* (verse 12) is *teko* in the Greek (Strong 2004). We get our English word *thaw* from it. *Webster's New Students Dictionary* (1969) defines thaw as "reversing the effect of freezing." Winter releases its grip when the spring thaw sets in. Corruption and death will one day release their grip on the world.

The picture Peter had in mind when he wrote of earth's future was one of transformation, not annihilation. The context in which he made his statement removes all doubt as to what he meant. Just before the apostle penned this declaration about earth's future, he referenced Noah's Flood. Peter stated, *"By water also the world of that time was deluged and destroyed"* (2 Peter 3:6, NIV). The worldwide Flood didn't destroy earth. Instead, the waters cleansed it of evil. And although the earth was changed by the onslaught of water, there was continuity between the pre-Flood and post-Flood world.

The great Flood brought a surface cleansing to the planet, but the root problem—the plague of death that enveloped creation when Adam sinned—was not addressed. That's still to come, and that purifying process will be accomplished by fire. This final cleansing flame won't be natural. Fire is often used figuratively in the Bible to describe the attributes and actions of Almighty God, including His spoken Word.

> *"Therefore, this is what the Lord God Almighty says* [to the prophet Jeremiah]: *'Because the people are talking* [sinfully], ***I will give you messages that will burn them up as if they were kindling wood'"*** (Jeremiah 5:14, NLT).

*"'Does not my word burn like fire?' asks the Lord.
'Is it not like a mighty hammer that smashes rock to
pieces?'"* (Jeremiah 23:29, NLT).

Almighty God is going to purge the material elements that
make up the physical world with the fire of His Word. Just like
in the beginning when God spoke and created the heavens and
the earth, He will speak again and atoms will literally be loosed
from their present state of corruption. They'll be put back
together in a new heavens and a new earth—the entire universe
released from captivity to decay and death.

Heaven and Earth Will Pass Away?

Some of you may be wondering, "Didn't Jesus say that the
heavens and the earth will pass away?" Although He uttered
these words, we must consider them in context. Jesus made this
statement several days before His crucifixion. His words were
part of an answer He gave to His followers when they asked
what signs will indicate that His return to this world is near. The
Lord listed a number of events and declared that the generation
that sees the beginning signs will witness them all.

*"Verily I say unto you, This generation shall not pass,
till all these things be fulfilled. Heaven and earth shall
pass away, but my words shall not pass away"* (Matthew 24:34-35, KJV).

Jesus wasn't informing these men that the world will someday
cease to exist. He was assuring them of the reliability of His
Word. He'd just made a number of predictive statements in
response to their question and concluded by saying His Word is
so reliable that the heavens and the earth will pass away before
it goes unfulfilled. These first-century men couldn't imagine

anything wiping out the earth, so they understood Jesus' point: nothing can stop God's Word from coming to pass. You and I aren't impacted by the Lord's comment in the same way as His original followers because we can envision the world being destroyed. We know all about nuclear weapons and their destructive power, and we've seen plenty of movies about asteroids hitting the planet.

Pilgrims Passing Through?

You may also be thinking, "Doesn't the Bible say this world is not our home and we're only pilgrims passing through?" Scripture does refer to believers as sojourners (1 Peter 2:11; Hebrews 11:13). However, those passages don't mean we're traveling through, never to return. The idea is that we're passing through the earth as it is—an earth bound by corruption and death. We'll come back to live here forever once the world has been cleansed and renewed.

REDEMPTION IS BIG!

Redemption is big enough to deliver both mankind and the earth from sin and its effects. If this surprises you, consider these thoughts.

- Jesus went to the Cross to destroy the works of the devil in mankind and in the earth, not to obliterate the people or the world He created. *The reason the Son of God was made manifest (visible) was to* **undo** *(destroy, loosen and dissolve) the works the devil [has done]"* (1 John 3:8, AMP). The word translated *undo* is the word *luo* or *"loose"* (Strong 2004).

- What kind of salvation would it be if the Lord was able to save men and women from sin and its effects and transform them into sons and daughters, but His plan wasn't big enough to save the family home?

This is God's world. *"The earth is the LORD's, and the fullness thereof"* (Psalm 24:1, KJV). He's not going to surrender one atom of His material creation to sin, Satan, corruption, or death. His redemption extends as far as the curse of sin and death is found. When Jesus Christ comes again, He'll complete the process of redemption by liberating all of creation from slavery to corruption and cleansing it from every trace of death.

> *"He* [Jesus] *was supreme in the beginning and— leading the resurrection parade—he is supreme in the end. From beginning to end he's there, towering far above everything, everyone. So spacious is he, so roomy, that everything of God finds its proper place in him without crowding. Not only that, but all the broken and dislocated pieces of the universe— people and things, animals and atoms—get properly fixed and fit together in vibrant harmonies, all because of his death, his blood that poured down from the Cross"* (Colossians 1:18-20, The Message).

⟶⟫⟩ · ⟨⟨⟨⟵

The Bible tells us that *"this world in its present form is passing away"* (1 Corinthians 7:31, NIV). But it assures us the heavens and the earth won't be destroyed. They will be reclaimed and redeemed from the effects of sin to become what God always intended—a perfect home for Himself and His family. Our forever home will be the earth we know and love.

WE WILL LIVE ON EARTH FOREVER

When Jesus came into this world two thousand years ago, He was born a Jew. All of His first followers were Old Covenant Jews. This meant, among other things, that their view of reality was shaped by the Law and the Prophets, or what we know as the Old Testament. These writings assured Peter, John, Paul, and the other disciples that their ultimate destiny (and ours) is to live on earth forever.

Old Covenant men and women knew that the Lord God will one day establish His visible kingdom here. They believed that death was a temporary departure from this world and expected their bodies to be raised from the grave so they can live forever in God's kingdom on earth. Although these people didn't know how or when they would return to earth, they were certain they would.

THEIR VIEW OF THE FUTURE

Peter the apostle was an ardent follower of Jesus. One day, he asked our Savior how he and the rest of the original twelve disciples would be rewarded for leaving everything to serve Him. Jesus replied:

*"Verily I say unto you, That ye which have followed me, in the **regeneration** when the Son of man shall sit in the throne of his glory, ye also shall sit upon twelve thrones, judging the twelve tribes of Israel. And every one that hath forsaken houses, or brethren, or sisters, or father, or mother, or wife, or children, or lands, for my name's sake, shall receive an hundredfold, and shall inherit everlasting life"* (Matthew 19:28-29, KJV).

The Lord told His men that their reward will come in the regeneration. The Greek word used here means "new birth" (Strong 2004): *"in the new age—the Messianic **rebirth** of the world"* (Matthew 19:28-29, AMP); *"at the **renewal** of all things"* (Matthew 19:28-29, NIV). Notice that Jesus didn't explain what He meant by the regeneration. He didn't need to because His disciples knew what He was talking about. Many Old Testament prophets wrote about the coming regeneration, or rebirth, of the world and Peter and the others were aware of their predictions.

Jesus assured them that they will have positions of great responsibility, get back over and above what they gave up to follow Him, and receive everlasting life. For most twenty-first century Christians, *everlasting life* means a wispy, ethereal existence in a shadowy spirit world where we float on clouds and play harps. But that's not what the term meant to these disciples. Based on the writings of the prophets, they would have understood everlasting life to mean: "Your body will be raised from the dead, so you can live on earth again; all that you've lost will be restored, and this time, you'll keep it forever; death can never again rob from you." I'll deal with these points more fully in upcoming chapters, but for now, consider several Old Testament passages that gave Peter and the others this hope.

*"I know that my Redeemer lives, and that in the end he will stand upon the earth. And **after my skin has been destroyed, yet in my flesh I will see God**"* (Job 19:25-26, NIV).

*"But **your dead will live; their bodies will rise.** You who dwell in the dust, wake up and shout for joy. Your dew is like the dew of the morning; **the earth will give birth to her dead**"* (Isaiah 26:19, NIV).

*"**But the meek [in the end] shall inherit the earth**"* (Psalm 37:11, AMP).

*"...The upright will have the earth for their heritage, **and will go on living there forever**"* (Psalm 37:29, <u>The Word</u> [Basic], p. 1021).

Transformation, Not Destruction

On an afternoon shortly after Jesus left this world, Peter and John went up to the Temple in Jerusalem. They encountered a lame man at the entrance and proceeded to heal him by the power of God in the name of Jesus. Temple-goers knew the suddenly cured man well, and a large crowd gathered to see what happened. Peter used this opportunity to proclaim Jesus' recent crucifixion and resurrection.

The apostle made a statement that sheds great light on his understanding of the future of this planet. Peter told the crowd that the Lord has gone back to Heaven where He will remain *"until the times of **restitution** of all things, which God hath spoken by the mouth of all his holy prophets since the world began"* (Acts 3:21, KJV). *Restitution* means "to restore something to its former state" (Strong 2004), or as one translator renders it, *"until the final recovery of all things from sin"* (Acts 3:21, TLB).

Peter reminded his audience that God has been talking about a time of restoration and recovery since earth's earliest days. Soon after Adam and Eve sinned and brought the curse of death to this world, Almighty God began to unveil His plan of redemption with the promise of a coming Redeemer (Genesis 3:15). As the years passed, the Lord revealed increasing aspects of this plan and instructed His prophets to record His Words in what became the Old Testament. These writers affirm that deliverance from sin and its effects is coming for both mankind and the earth.

Peter and the others knew from what God's spokesmen had written that the Lord God is working to reclaim what was lost when Adam sinned—His family and the home He made for us. Based on the Old Testament writings, the people who lived and walked with Jesus in the first century expected the Lord to restore Eden, or Paradise, on earth. These concepts were undoubtedly reinforced by talks with Jesus in the three years He was with them. The prophets go on to reveal the effect on God's creation when He comes to restore this world: Bodies resurrected and renewed. Wildernesses restored. Barren, dry places made lush. Troublesome weeds banished. Peace and joy abounding.

> *"The LORD will surely comfort Zion and will look with compassion on all her ruins;* ***he will make her deserts like Eden, her wastelands like the garden of the Lord"*** (Isaiah 51:3, NIV).

> *"The desert and the parched land will be glad;* ***the wilderness will rejoice and blossom****. Like the crocus,*

it will burst into bloom…water will gush forth in the wilderness and streams in the desert. The burning sand will become a pool, the thirsty ground bubbling springs" (Isaiah 35:1-7, NIV).

"You will live in joy and peace. The mountains and hills will burst into song, and the trees of the field will clap their hands! Where once there were thorns, cypress trees will grow. Where briars grew, myrtles will sprout up" (Isaiah 55:12-13, NLT).

A NEW EARTH

Peter and the rest of Jesus' early followers expected the entire material universe—both the heavens and the earth—to be made new. This revelation was first given to Isaiah the prophet seven hundred years before Jesus came into the world. The Lord God declared: *"For, behold, I create **new heavens and a new earth**, and the former things shall not be remembered or come into mind"* (Isaiah 65:17, AMP). Peter actually referenced this prophecy immediately following his statement that the earth will be changed (2 Peter 3:10-12).

*"But we look for **new heavens and a new earth** according to His promise, in which righteousness (uprightness, freedom from sin, and right standing with God) is to abide"* (2 Peter 3:13, AMP).

In this passage, Peter used a very specific Greek word for *new* when he wrote of earth's future: *kainos*. The word means "new in quality or form" as opposed to "new in time" (Vine 1984). This same word is used to describe a person who has been born again through faith in Christ: *"Therefore if any man be in Christ, he is a **new** creature"* (2 Corinthians 5:17, KJV).

- The new birth doesn't turn people into something that never existed before. The new birth transforms the one who has believed on Jesus by flooding their innermost being with eternal life.

- Just as a new creature is the same person transformed, the new heavens and earth will be this earth (along with the atmosphere and expanse around and above us) changed by eternal life and made new in quality and superior in character.

No Memory of Earth?

Before proceeding, I want to deal with a concern that may arise at this point. Isaiah's prophecy is sometimes used to support the idea that in Heaven, we won't remember anything or anyone from our life on earth. But the prophet said nothing like that. His words were originally directed to real people in a desperate situation and were intended to give them hope. Isaiah prophesied to a remnant of men and women who remained faithful to Almighty God when the rest of their country became involved in willful, persistent idol worship and refused to repent. The nation of Israel was about to experience severe consequences because of this behavior. Through Isaiah, the Lord assured His loyal followers that one day, on the new earth, all will be made right and the hardships generated by their rebellious fellow countrymen will be a distant memory.

God promised these people: *"I will put aside my anger and forget the evil of earlier days"* (Isaiah 65:16, NLT). This sentence sets the context for Isaiah's comment that past things won't be remembered anymore. The forgetting is something the Lord will do. Because Almighty God is Omniscient (All-Knowing), He doesn't forget things in the sense that He's no longer aware of them. Instead, He chooses not to recall them. That's the idea in Isaiah 65:17. The Lord assured His people that when the world is made new, this ugly period in their history would be forgiven and forgotten. Isaiah's prophecy has nothing to do with us not remembering our relationships or life experiences.

Humanity's history won't be erased in the life to come. The transformation of earth is the beginning of another chapter in this planet's history. In fact, many of us will be more interested in earth's past than we've ever been because we'll view it through the perspective of redemption completed. We'll learn how God worked in the affairs of men in a fallen world and caused everything to serve His eternal purposes.

John Saw the New Earth

As part of his visit to Heaven, the apostle John saw the new heavens and earth in a vision. He recorded what he witnessed in the Book of Revelation. He saw a world that was transformed, not annihilated. His opening statement makes this evident: *"I saw a **new** heaven and a **new** earth: for the **first** heaven and first earth were passed away"* (Revelation 21:1, KJV).

- John used the same Greek word for *new* that Peter did. He employed the word again several verses later when, in the context of what he was observing, he wrote that he heard God declare, *"Behold, I make all things **new"*** (Revelation 21:5, KJV). The Lord didn't say He makes all new things. He said He makes what already exists new in quality and superior in character.

- John called our present world the first heavens and earth. First is the Greek word *protos*, which means "first in time or place" (Strong 2004). We can see the root of our English term *prototype* in this word. A *prototype* is "an original model on which something else is patterned" *(Webster's New Students Dictionary 1969).* This present world is the pattern for the one to come.

• John reported that the first earth had passed away. Once again, he selected the same word Peter chose when he wrote *"the heavens shall pass away"* (2 Peter 3:10, KJV). Remember, this Greek term carries the idea of passing from one condition to another. The apostle Paul also utilized this word when he described a man or woman born of God as a new creature. He stated that *"the old (previous moral and spiritual condition) has passed away. Behold, the fresh and new has come"* (2 Corinthians 5:17, AMP). The one who believes on Jesus doesn't cease to be. Rather, he is transformed inwardly by eternal life.

· →⟫⟫⟩ · ⟨⟪⟪← ·

Jesus' original followers understood their future better than many of us do today. They knew from the Word of God, given through His prophets, that this world won't be destroyed. It will be renovated. And they were aware that there will be continuity between the old and new earth. The best of earth, even in its fallen condition, gives a fleeting glimpse of what's ahead.

This planet has been corrupted by man's sin but will be reclaimed, redeemed, and restored to become what Almighty God always intended, a perfect home for Himself and His family. It will be earth—the earth we know and love—cleansed but recognizable, new but familiar.

THE CAPITAL OF HEAVEN ON EARTH

In the Book of Revelation, John reported that he witnessed the culmination of the plan of redemption: Almighty God coming to live with His family in the home He made for us. John saw the capital city of Heaven descending out of the invisible realm to the new earth and heard a voice proclaim that God's home is now with men.

> *"Then I saw a new heaven and a new earth...And I saw* **the holy city, the new Jerusalem,** *coming down from God out of heaven like a beautiful bride prepared for her husband. I heard a loud shout from the throne, saying, 'Look,* **the home of God is now among his people! He will live with them, and they will be his people.** *God himself will be with them. He will remove all of their sorrows, and there will be no more death or sorrow or crying or pain. For the old world and its evils are gone forever"* (Revelation 21:1-4, NLT).

Many misconceptions about the life awaiting us come from misinterpretations of what John went on to describe about the city. From his depiction, some have concluded that earth is going to be replaced by a cube-shaped, multi-layered, transparent city

101

where we'll live forever with no sun, moon, or sea. This doesn't sound very inviting to those of us who would prefer a log home and a campfire on a moonlit night or a beachfront home and a sunny day to a mansion in a see-through city.

For a moment, let's put aside any preconceived ideas we may have about John's account and think about what it would have meant to the people John originally wrote to in the first century. Doing so will help us discard erroneous beliefs about our future home.

THE CITY JOHN SAW

John's vision opened with a scene beautiful beyond description—a city glowing with and illuminated by the glory of God come to earth.

> *"The holy city, Jerusalem...was filled with the glory of God and sparkled like a precious gem, crystal clear like jasper. Its walls were broad and high, with twelve gates...three gates on each side—east, north, south, and west"* (Revelation 21:10-13, NLT).

> *"The wall was made of jasper, and the city was pure gold, as clear as glass. The wall of the city was built on foundation stones inlaid with twelve gems* [jasper, sapphire, agate, emerald, onyx, carnelian, chrysolite, beryl, topaz, chrysoprase, jacinth, amethyst]. *The twelve gates were made of pearls—each gate from a single pearl! And the main street was pure gold, as clear as glass"* (Revelation 21:18-21, NLT).

God's Dwelling Place

John's original readers understood that the city was glowing, bejeweled, and golden—not because it's freaky or otherworldly, but because it is the home of God. They were familiar with the writings of the prophets who reported several instances where Heaven briefly opened to people on earth. In each case, men saw brilliant light and precious stones as the Lord, in all His glory, appeared before them. Here are two examples:

> *"Then Moses, Aaron, Nadab, Abihu, and seventy of the leaders of Israel went up the mountain. There they saw the God of Israel. Under his feet there seemed to be a pavement of brilliant sapphire, as clear as the heavens"* (Exodus 24:9-10, NLT).

> *"[I, Ezekiel, saw] what looked like a throne made of blue sapphire. And high above this throne was a figure whose appearance was like that of a man. From his waist up, he looked like gleaming amber, flickering like a fire. And from his waist down, he looked like a burning flame, shining with splendor. All around him was a glowing halo, like a rainbow shining through the clouds. This was the way the glory of the LORD appeared to me"* (Ezekiel 1:26-28, NLT).

John's audience was not put off by his report of a golden city because they were familiar with Solomon's Temple. The Temple was designed to be a fitting place for the Lord to meet with His people and, in keeping with this purpose, had an abundance of gold throughout (Exodus 25:10-40; 1 Kings 6:14-37). John's readers recognized that the city he saw come from Heaven is filled with gold because it's the dwelling place of Almighty God.

In his account of what he saw, John reported that the Lord's capital is *pure gold, as clear as glass*, and sparkles like *crystal clear jasper*. Some have wrongly taken John's description to mean the city is transparent. But think about it. When we describe a surface as being clear as glass, we mean it has no flaws or impurities. The gold in New Jerusalem is flawless, not see-through. When we speak of a crystal clear day, we don't mean that the sky is see-through. We mean there are no clouds to block its vibrant blue color. There is some dispute about exactly what type of stone jasper is, but it "seems to denote a translucent [shining, glowing] stone of various colors especially that of fire" (Vine 1984). Whatever jasper is, in this breathtaking city, the glory of God shines through like a luminary since there are no blemishes or imperfections in the gold or gemstones to obscure the brilliance of His glory.

Measuring the City

As the vision continued, John watched an angel measure the great metropolis. His measurements show that the city is in the shape of a cube, fourteen hundred miles in length, width, and height (Revelation 21:15-17). This detail didn't seem odd to those who first heard John's report. They were aware that in the Temple that stood in the city of Jerusalem in their day, the innermost room where God's glory appeared was cube-shaped (1 Kings 6:20). New Jerusalem is shaped like a cube because it is the Lord's home.

Some modern scholars maintain that the angel's measurements have symbolic meaning, but John wrote that *"the angel used a standard human measure"* (Revelation 21:17, NLT). Although the measurements indicate that the height of the city is higher than the present atmosphere of earth, the new earth may be bigger than the present planet. And God can certainly extend the atmosphere if He desires. Are there different levels in the city? How tall are its buildings? The Bible doesn't say. We'll find out when we see this heavenly capital.

The fact that an angel measured the city was very significant to men and women familiar with the Old Testament. They were aware that the prophet Zechariah saw an angel measure the earthly city of Jerusalem in one of his visions. In Zechariah's day, the once powerful nation of Israel had been reduced to an insignificant remnant under foreign control. Jerusalem was in ruins due to an enemy invasion, but this man of God prophesied that the Lord would one day restore the city. His vision brought great comfort and hope to his generation and to each succeeding generation down to John's day. The prophet wrote:

> *"He* [the angel] *replied, 'I am going to measure Jerusalem, to see how wide and how long it is'...The other angel said, 'Hurry, and say to that young man, 'Jerusalem will someday be so full of people that it won't have room enough for everyone! Many will live outside the city walls, with all their livestock—and yet they will be safe. For I, myself, will be a wall of fire around Jerusalem, says the Lord. And I will be the glory inside the city'"* (Zechariah 2:2-5, NLT).

At that time in history, walls were vital to a city for protection. The gates were closed in the face of danger as well as at night to ensure safety. Zechariah foresaw a time when city gates can remain open because Almighty God is present with His people. This is what John described—a heavenly city glowing with the glory of God that never closes its gates because all enemies

105

of the Lord and His people have been vanquished (Revelation 21:25).

The people to whom John's message was first given didn't interpret this information as unearthly or uninviting. They heard, "God in all His glory is coming to live with us and the arrival of His great city will mean peace, provision, and safety on earth." All will be made right. No more danger, loss, or death.

A Great River

The apostle John reported that he saw a great river flowing from God's throne in the center of New Jerusalem. *"And the angel showed me a pure river with the water of life, clear as crystal, flowing from the throne of God and of the Lamb, coursing down the center of the main street. On each side of the river grew a tree of life, bearing twelve crops of fruit, with a fresh crop each month"* (Revelation 22:1-2, NLT). John's readers knew from the writings of the prophets that when the Lord comes to live with His people, He will bring water to dry places.

- Isaiah predicted *"The deserts will become as green as the mountains of Lebanon"* (Isaiah 35:2, NLT).

- Zechariah, in the context of the Redeemer on earth, wrote, *"On that day life-giving waters will flow out from Jerusalem, half toward the Dead Sea and half toward the Mediterranean, flowing continuously both in summer and in winter"* (Zechariah 14:8, NLT).

- Ezekiel described a scene very similar to what John saw, a time in the future when the Lord God will be on earth with His people. *"All kinds of fruit trees will grow along both sides of the river. The leaves of these trees will never turn brown and fall, and there will always be fruit on their branches. There will be a new crop every month, without fail! For they are watered by the river flowing from the Temple"* (Ezekiel 47:12, NLT).

Ancient people who lived in arid climates without fresh water continually available would have been awed by the thought of a river of fresh, pure water flowing from God's Temple. None of this would have sounded weird. It sounded wonderful.

A Real City from Heaven

I realize that it's difficult to set aside preconceived ideas when we read what John wrote. Consequently, what he describes seems otherworldly and ethereal. But the apostle said he saw a city come out of Heaven. Remember, both he and Paul (two eyewitnesses of Heaven) reported that earth is patterned after heavenly realities and that objects on earth give us an idea of what God's home looks like. Therefore, it's reasonable to conclude that a city coming out of Heaven would in some way resemble cities on earth.

Hear John's information as if he described a spectacular urban center somewhere on earth. What images would your mind draw up? You'd probably envision people, residences, businesses, cultural activities, education, arts and entertainment, athletic events, parks, museums, restaurants, libraries, and concerts. John referenced a beautiful river coursing through this glowing metropolis. Because of the size of the city, the river probably has numerous tributaries. There are most likely waterfalls, ponds, and lakes in and around the area. Imagine people sitting, walking, and enjoying themselves beside these beautiful waterways. There is no reason to think these elements aren't present in the greatest city of all—the city of the Great King.

ONE GIANT CITY?

Some have mistakenly interpreted John's description of New Jerusalem to mean that the new earth will consist of this giant city and nothing else. John wasn't describing the entire planet in his account. He was picturing one location. Heaven's capital doesn't replace the world. It simply relocates here. A careful reading of the text in the last two chapters of Revelation reveals that there is more to the new earth than just one city.

- John wrote that when he saw New Jerusalem come out of Heaven he was standing on a mountain. *"So he [an angel] took me in spirit to a great, high mountain, and he showed me the holy city, Jerusalem, descending out of heaven from God"* (Revelation 21:10, NLT). Note that he called it *a* mountain as opposed to *the* mountain, suggesting there are other summits besides this one.

- In his vision, John saw rulers from around the world coming to the capital, which indicates there are other places on the new earth. *"The nations shall walk by its light and the rulers and leaders of the earth shall bring into it their glory...They shall bring the glory—the splendor and majesty—and the honor of the nations into [the city]"* (Revelation 21:24-26, AMP).

The idea that our future home consists of a single, giant, cube-shaped, transparent city would never have occurred to men and women familiar with what the Old Testament discloses about the life to come. Because of the words of the prophets, John's contemporaries were looking forward to beautiful landscapes with trees, vegetation, and flowers. Through His spokesmen, God promised to make a renewed earth, not a different earth.

- First-century people expected the Lord to restore the conditions of Eden. The Book of Genesis gives a description of the Garden, providing a hint of what our home will look like once it's freed from the effects of sin and made new. Not only was there lush greenery, Eden possessed gold, aromatic resin, and onyx, indicating various kinds of land formations and landscapes or what we call natural wonders (Genesis 2:10-14).

- John referred to this current world as the first earth, or prototype, of what's ahead (Revelation 21:1). Therefore, we can be assured that the new earth will resemble this planet as we know it, with all the wonder and beauty it possesses even in its present sin damaged condition.

NO SEA? NO SUN? NO MOON?

The apostle made two statements that have been wrongly interpreted to mean that the sun, moon, and sea will be absent from our forever home.

> *"And I saw a new heaven and a new earth: for the first heaven and the first earth were passed away; and there was no more sea"* (Revelation 21:1, KJV).

> *"And the city had no need of the sun, neither of the moon, to shine in it: for the glory of God did lighten it, and the Lamb is the light thereof"* (Revelation 21:23, KJV).

Once again, we must consider what these words meant to

the original readers. They realized John wasn't describing some sunless place with no sea. They understood he was writing about the earth they knew and loved released from corruption and restored to Eden-like conditions.

No More Sea?

When we hear no more sea, our first thought may be no more beachside vacations or ocean cruises. John's readers would have had a different reaction. In his day, the sea was a formidable obstacle, an enemy capable of great destruction. Sailors traveled the waves in wooden ships with no radar or navigation equipment to guide them around storms and submerged obstacles. Sailing away from the shoreline meant risking death. Even though residual waters from Noah's Flood cover two-thirds of the globe, you and I can hop into a jumbo jet and safely cross the oceans in a matter of hours. That was unimaginable in John's time.

When John wrote *"no more sea,"* he meant no more sea as we know it. As with every other part of creation, the oceans have been damaged by sin, but they will be reclaimed and restored when Jesus returns. Scripture reveals that there will be large bodies of water on the new earth. Note these points:

- God created seas. They pre-date sin and are part of the home He made for His family. *"And God said, 'Let the waters beneath the sky be gathered into one place so dry ground may appear.' And so it was. God named the dry ground 'land' and the waters 'seas.' And God saw that it was good"* (Genesis 1:9-10, NLT).

- The Bible says that a great river flowed out of Eden and then separated into four large rivers (Genesis 2:10). Rivers must flow into something, implying that there were large bodies of water on earth before man sinned.

- The prophet Isaiah, in his description of the new earth, mentioned seas, ships, and islands. *"The wealth on the seas will be brought to you"* (Isaiah 60:5, NIV). *"Surely the islands look to me; in the lead are the ships of Tarshish"* (Isaiah 60:9, NIV).

- The river that John saw in New Jerusalem flows somewhere, suggesting a great body of water on the new earth (Revelation 22:1).

- The present earth (or prototype) has large lakes that are actually freshwater oceans. It's unlikely that they'll be lost when the earth is redeemed from corruption and death.

No More Sun or Moon?

John never said there will be no sun or moon on the new earth. He said their light isn't needed in the capital because the brilliant light of God's glory is visibly present in the city. Men who have seen the glory of God describe it as brighter than the sun's light (Acts 26:13).

For the people in antiquity, the idea that darkness will be banished was fantastic news. Nighttime isn't ominous to us because we live in the age of electricity. Even when it's dark, it's not truly dark. We can't appreciate what nightfall meant before electric lighting was developed. To be outside your home or beyond the city gates after sunset meant great danger. When the world is made new, however, there will be nothing that hurts or harms in any way, including unrelenting darkness. The fact that the *"[city] gates never close at the end of day because there is no night"* was a tremendous promise that inspired hope in the hearts of John's readers (Revelation 21:25, NLT).

While there'll be no night in the capital city, there will be night elsewhere on the new earth. Otherwise, we won't be able to see the moon and the stars, the planets and the galaxies. The Lord placed them all there for us to observe and enjoy.

· →》》》 · 《《《← ·

John's readers heard his words in the context of God's promise to deliver creation from bondage to sin, corruption, and death and restore earth to a fit forever home for Himself and His family. They would have received the apostle's vision as a reminder that the Lord keeps His promise and His plan of redemption will one day be completed. They knew the life ahead is gain, not loss.

John's record isn't the only description of what's in store for us and this planet. The Bible reveals a lot more information about our future home. Let's delve into it.

WHAT THE PROPHETS SAY ABOUT THE NEW EARTH

*J*ohn's vision of the new earth focuses on just one city, the New Jerusalem. He wasn't given many details about the rest of the planet. We must turn to the writings of the Old Testament prophets for additional information about our future home. They make it clear that earth won't be foreign to us. The prophets paint a picture of a world that is new but familiar, changed but recognizable. God's spokesmen reveal that there will be continuity in both appearance and activity on the new earth.

NEW BUT FAMILIAR

In the previous chapter, I discussed how misinterpretations of John's description of the capital city cause some people to erroneously envision the new earth as a strange, cube-shaped, transparent world made of gold and crystal with no sun or moon. But the Old Testament writers report the Lord's original design for the heavens and the earth is going to be retained.

- The prophets Haggai and Zechariah tell us in a psalm they wrote that the sun, moon, and stars will last forever. *"Praise him, sun and moon! Praise him, all you twinkling stars! Praise him, skies above! Praise him, vapors high above the clouds...for* [the Lord] *issued his command, and they came into being.* **He established them forever and forever. His orders will never be revoked"** (Psalm 148:3-6, NLT).

- King David of Israel recorded a prayer he prayed for his son and successor Solomon. In the midst of the prayer, David began to prophesy about Jesus coming to earth to reign as King. The prophecy depicts a world we'll recognize with sky, sun, moon, rivers, seas, coastlines, and islands.

"May they fear you Lord, as long as the **sun** *shines, as long as the* **moon** *continues in the* **skies***. Yes, forever!...May he* [Jesus] *reign from* **sea** *to* **sea***, and from the* **Euphrates River** *to the ends of the earth"* (Psalm 72:5-8, NLT).

"Kings along the **Mediterranean Coast**—*the kings of Tarshish and the* **islands**—*and those from Sheba and from Seba* [in Arabia]—*all will bring their gifts. Yes, kings from everywhere! All will bow before him* [Jesus]*! All will serve him* (Psalm 72:10, TLB).

Other Old Testament spokesmen disclose that earth will still look like earth, and God's family will engage in familiar activities. These prophets wrote about men and women who build houses, plant vineyards, harvest crops, and interact with friends and loved ones at feasts with food, drink, laughter, and conversation (see note 6).

"Look! I am creating new heavens and a new earth...Be glad; rejoice forever in my creation...In those days, **people will live in the houses they build and eat the fruit of their own vineyards***"* (Isaiah 65:17-21, NLT).

"Everyone will live quietly in their own homes in peace and prosperity, for there will be nothing to fear" (Micah 4:4, NLT). *"Each of you will invite your neighbor into your home to share your peace and prosperity"* (Zechariah 3:10, NLT).

"'The time will come,' says the Lord, 'when the grain and the grapes will grow faster than they can be harvested...[My people] will plant vineyards and gardens; they will eat their crops and drink their wine'" (Amos 9:13-14, NLT).

"On this mountain the LORD Almighty will prepare a feast of rich food for all peoples, a banquet of aged wine...On this mountain he will destroy the shroud that enfolds all peoples, the sheet that covers all nations; he will swallow up death forever. The Sovereign Lord will wipe away the tears from all faces" (Isaiah 25:6-8, NIV).

CREATION RESTORED

Possibly you're thinking, "This can't be right! It sounds too normal and non-spiritual to be our forever life." But we were created for such things. And God's aim in redemption is to recover what He purposed from the beginning—before sin damaged both the family and our home. Therefore, we can get an idea of how the renewed world will look as well as what we'll do by examining earth before it was corrupted.

The prophet Moses gives us much information about the pre-sin creation in the opening passages of the Book of Genesis. He recorded that the Lord God fashioned a world with seas and sky and land covered with grasses, plants, and fruit-bearing trees.

115

God filled humanity's dwelling place with birds, animals, and sea creatures of every sort and He surrounded earth with the sun, moon, and stars. None of this will be destroyed. Instead, it will be renovated and become a rejuvenated version of what Almighty God created in the beginning.

Cultivating the Land

The Lord designed human beings to engage in meaningful, satisfying work. When we read what Moses wrote about Adam in the Garden of Eden, it's apparent that cultivation of the earth was part of God's original plan for man before sin.

> *"Now the LORD God had planted a garden in the east, in Eden; and there he put the man he had formed. And the LORD God made all kinds of trees grow out of the ground—trees that were pleasing to the eye and good for food...* **The Lord God took the man and put him in the Garden of Eden to work it and take care of it**" (Genesis 2:8-15, NIV).

God created the plant kingdom in a state of maturity so that a harvest was available when man came on the scene. Since the Garden produced spontaneously, Adam had to maintain it to prevent profuse growth. But there's another reason God commissioned Adam to tend the Garden. The Lord God set up a finite system with an infinite source of supply to provide food for His family: *"And God said, 'Look! I have given you the* **seed-bearing plants** *throughout the earth and all the fruit trees for your food'"* (Genesis 1:29, NLT). Seed-bearing plants can potentially yield fruit, vegetables, and grains forever if, when the last ear of corn is eaten, you sow the seed to produce another crop. In other words, in a limited system with an endless supply source, somebody (like Adam) has to plant and harvest.

116

Sowing and reaping require related activities such as producing necessary tools and appropriate clothing, constructing houses and storage buildings, and devising systems for distribution and preparation of the land's yield. All of this developed as Adam and Eve began to have children and earth's population increased. It's no surprise that the prophets foresaw farming, houses, families, and feasts when earth is made new and the conditions of Eden are restored. This was the Lord's plan from the start.

Time and Seasons on the New Earth

The fact that human beings are going to farm means we'll need to keep track of time in our forever home since a finite system with an infinite supply source involves a cycle of planting and harvesting. The continued existence of the sun and moon is further evidence that time will forever be part of our lives. These heavenly bodies have served this purpose since the world began.

> *"And God said, Let there be lights in the expanse of the heavens to separate the day from the night; and let them be for signs and tokens [of God's provident care],* **and [to mark] seasons, days, and years** *"* (Genesis 1:14, AMP).

But there's more to it. In his description of earth before sin, Moses recorded that the lights in the heavens were given—not only to keep track of days and years, but to mark seasons. He further reported that seasons will last as long as the earth does: *"While the earth remaineth, seedtime and harvest, and* **cold** *and* **heat**, *and* **summer** *and* **winter**, *and day and night* **shall not cease** *"* (Genesis 8:22, KJV).

I've had people challenge me on the idea that there will be seasons on the new earth. Most of their objections come from books and articles written by creationists—men and women in the scientific community who believe the biblical account of creation. Many of them have written extensively about the geological and meteorological makeup of earth prior to Adam's sin and the Flood. I find these writings fascinating and love to read them myself.

A number of creation scientists are convinced that in those early days, a large canopy of water vapor surrounded the entire planet. They believe this canopy produced a powerful greenhouse effect that resulted in a consistent, pleasant, warm climate worldwide. They also maintain that these conditions will be restored when the world is renewed, bringing an end to the seasonal variations presently experienced on earth. Although I appreciate their point of view, the Bible says that as long as the earth remains there will be seasons. Recently, some creationists have revised their opinions on this subject (see note 7).

Again, we must remember the big picture: God is working to restore the home He made for His family, and seasons are part of His original provision for His sons and daughters. Due to the effects of Adam's sin, certain aspects of the seasons are currently challenging for mankind. The curse of corruption in the earth produces colliding air masses that trigger disastrous storms. This results in extremes of heat and cold that bring crop-shriveling droughts in summer and sheets of road-coating ice in winter. When earth is renewed, Almighty God can certainly recreate a cycle of seasons that doesn't involve these destructive and sometimes deadly weather excesses. Once corruption is removed, the climatic variations will no longer be catastrophic. Seasons will be a source of pleasure just as they were before sin.

Even though I cannot explain every aspect of life on the new earth, we can't let what we don't know undermine what we do know. God's Word is definitive. Whatever is ahead is gain, not loss—better, not worse. Every season has its beauty. Who doesn't relish a crisp autumn morning and the spectacle of the leaves turning colors? Who hasn't delighted in a wintry wonderland created by a gentle overnight snow? If we lose these kinds of wonders in our future home, is the new earth really better than the old?

The Blessing of Rainfall

Although the Bible doesn't give a lot of specific details about earth's climate before Adam sinned, it seems that the Lord intended rainfall to be part of the process of raising crops. A passage in Genesis suggests as much. Note the connection between crops, rain, and man.

> *"This is the account of the heavens and the earth when they were created, in the day that the LORD God made earth and heaven. Now no shrub of the field was yet in the earth, and no plant of the field had yet sprouted, for **the LORD God had not sent rain upon the earth, and there was no man to cultivate the ground**"* (Genesis 2:4-5, NASB).

Obviously, the cycle that creates rain has been negatively affected by the consequences of Adam's sin, resulting in torrential rains and flooding. Although rain can lead to destruction, many Bible passages speak of rain as a blessing from God. When the earth is released from its bondage to corruption and death, rainfall will again fulfill its created purpose and be a blessing to mankind.

> *"Nevertheless* [God] *left not himself without witness,*
> *in that he did good, and gave us rain from heaven,*
> *and fruitful seasons, filling our hearts with food and*
> *gladness"* (Acts 14:17, KJV).

> "[God] *covers the heavens with clouds, provides*
> *rain for the earth, and makes the green grass grow in*
> *mountain pastures"* (Psalm 147:8, NLT).

Even though these Old Testament prophets lived centuries ago, they still speak to us. Their words give us valuable information about life after death. Our forever home won't be otherworldly. It will be the earth we know and love, delivered from the curse of corruption and death and restored to be what Almighty God always planned. According to the Lord's spokesmen, there will be continuity between this life and the life to come. Not only will the landscapes and scenery feel like home, we'll also engage in familiar activities. In the next few chapters, we'll take a closer look at what men and women will do on the new earth.

NATIONS, CULTURES, AND CIVILIZATIONS ON THE NEW EARTH

*T*alk of Eden being re-established on earth can give the impression that we'll go back to wearing fig leaves, picking fruit off trees, and sleeping in pine needle beds on the ground. But these images of our future are contrary to what God's Word declares. Life will be new but familiar, changed but recognizable, due to the fact that nations, cultures, and civilizations will continue on the new earth.

NATIONS AND NATIONALITIES

Ethnic identity is part of our God-given uniqueness. All the various people groups on earth were in Adam when God created him: *"And He made from one [common origin, one source, one blood] all **nations** of men to settle on the face of the earth"* (Acts 17:26, AMP). The Greek word translated *nation* means "multitude, people, race, belonging and living together" (Strong 2004). These national distinctions persist after death.

- The apostle John witnessed different ethnicities and nationalities when he visited Heaven. *"After this I looked and there before me was a great multitude that no one could*

121

*count, from every **nation, tribe, people and language**, standing before the throne"* (Revelation 7:9, NIV).

- John also observed distinct people groups on the new earth. He referred to them as nations and mentioned that their leaders come to earth's capital, New Jerusalem. *"The **nations** of the earth will walk in its light* [the capital], *and the **rulers** of the world will come* [to the city]*"* (Revelation 21:24, NLT).

A Kingdom of Kingdoms

Jesus Christ is coming back to establish His visible kingdom on earth. His kingdom will be a domain made up of kingdoms submitted to His rulership. Scripture reveals that Jesus will rule over people who reign.

- The Old Testament prophets predicted this: *"He* [the Lord] *will rule from sea to sea and from the River* [Euphrates] *to the ends of the earth...The **kings** of Tarshish and of distant shores will bring tribute to him...All **kings** will bow down to him and all **nations** will serve him"* (Psalm 72:8-11, NIV).

- John saw it in his vision: *"The **kingdoms** of this world are become the **kingdoms** of our Lord, and of his Christ; and he shall reign for ever and ever"* (Revelation 11:15, KJV).

- John further noted that the numerous ethnic groups he witnessed in Heaven look forward to returning to earth to rule. He heard them sing, *"*[You, Jesus, have] *redeemed us to God by thy blood out of every kindred, and tongue, and people, and nation...and we shall **reign on the earth**"* (Revelation 5:9-10, KJV).

REIGNING ON EARTH

When the Lord sets up His kingdom, He is going to give rulership positions to some of the redeemed as part of their reward for faithful service to Him. However, reigning on earth involves more than this. The great Old Testament prophet Daniel was given lots of information about the establishment of God's visible rule on earth. He foresaw that when Jesus takes control of this world, His redeemed people will be given the dominion and greatness of its kingdoms.

> *"But the saints of the Most High [God] shall receive the kingdom, and possess the kingdom for ever, even for ever and ever"* (Daniel 7:18, AMP).

> *"And the **kingdom** and the **dominion** and the greatness of the kingdom under the whole heavens shall be given to the people of the saints of the Most High; His kingdom is an everlasting kingdom, and all the dominions shall serve and obey Him"* (Daniel 7:27, AMP).

Made for Dominion

To fully grasp what dominion means for life on the new earth, we must once again go back to the beginning. The Bible opens with Almighty God creating humankind in His image: *"And God said, Let us make man in our image, after our likeness: and let them have **dominion**"* (Genesis 1:26, KJV). *Dominion* comes from a word that means "to rule or to subjugate" (Strong 2004). We tend to think of this rulership only in terms of holding sway over Satan or other people.

- Ruling over Satan is not part of our created purpose. It's

123

a sub-purpose in this life necessitated by the evil one's rebellion and Adam's fall. There will be no devil to reign over in our future home since he'll be forever removed from human contact (Revelation 20:10).

* Dominion also has nothing to do with reigning over people. There were no other people when Adam and Eve received authority. The fact is, the entire human race was resident in Adam when God issued His dominion command. Rulership was conferred on all human beings at the same time in Adam.

Dominion actually refers to mankind's relationship with the rest of creation. This becomes clear when we read the entire verse.

* After the Lord God bestowed dominion on humanity he decreed, *"And let them rule over the fish of the sea and the birds of the air, over the livestock, over all the earth, and over all the creatures that move along the ground"* (Genesis 1:26, NIV).

* The psalmist David was inspired to state the Lord's command this way: *"You put us in charge of everything you made, giving us authority over all things—the sheep and the cattle and all the wild animals, the birds in the sky, the fish in the sea, and everything that swims the ocean currents"* (Psalm 8:6-8, NLT).

The Genesis passage goes on to report that after God conferred dominion on mankind, His first instructions to Adam and Eve pertained to interaction with this world. The Lord commanded them to begin the tasks of populating and subduing the earth: *"Be **fruitful, multiply**, and **fill the earth** and **subdue** it [with all* *its vast resources]"* (Genesis 1:28, AMP).

To be fruitful and multiply means to have children. To subdue the earth involves bringing creation into subjection by using and enjoying its resources. This is exactly what the Lord immediately directed the man and the woman to do. He authorized them to utilize the natural produce of earth for food: *"I have given you the seed-bearing plants throughout the earth and all the fruit trees for your food"* (Genesis 1:29, NLT).

Subduing the Earth

Adam and Eve obeyed the Lord's command to multiply (Genesis 4:1). As the family grew, they and their offspring exercised dominion and began to subdue the earth. They utilized its resources and produced cultures and civilizations.

- These first people farmed, herded livestock, and manufactured tents and musical instruments. They developed metallurgy, ventured out on the seas, and discovered new lands. Men devised governments and built cities and empires. Adam's many sons and daughters invented furnace-dried brick for erecting great buildings and learned to work with bitumen (Genesis 4:20-22; Genesis 11:2-4).

- From those earliest days down to the present time, each succeeding generation of mankind has, in some manner, reigned over and subdued the earth by using its bounty to produce a way of life for themselves.

Every culture and civilization established on earth since the dawn of man has common elements. All build shelters, gather food, plant and harvest crops, and make things. Every people group practices food storage and preparation. Each one produces clothing, jewelry, music, and art. All create and tell stories and preserve memories. They decorate their homes and have celebrations. These activities are expressions of humankind fulfilling part of their created purpose: to reign over and subdue the earth by using its resources.

Human creativity has produced some marvelous things through the centuries from beautiful paintings and musical compositions to industrial and technological products. Regrettably, much of what we've developed has been used for evil in this sin cursed world. Overall, fallen mankind has failed to produce God-glorifying civilizations. But this problem will be rectified on the new earth. In connection with the establishment of His everlasting kingdom on earth, the Lord will cleanse and purify human culture so it does what it was always intended to do—glorify Him and bless His family.

Cultures and Civilizations on the New Earth

You may recall that Peter the apostle compared the coming transformation of the world with Noah's Flood (2 Peter 3:6). The waters didn't destroy earth; they cleansed and changed it. Neither did the flood alter God's purposes for humanity. Noah and his family were preserved in the ark so they could return to earth. The Lord's first command to them after the deluge subsided was the same one He gave Adam and Eve: *"Replenish the earth and have dominion over it"* (Genesis 9:1, The Word [Septuagint], p. 11). Noah obeyed and *"began farming and planted a vineyard"* (Genesis 9:20, NASB). There was continuity from the pre-Flood to the post-Flood world. Cultural information was not lost. It carried on.

So it will be when Jesus returns. Mankind won't start from

scratch on the new earth. Cultural developments that were sinful are going to be eliminated. Those that were not sinful but used for wicked purposes or by people with evil motives will be purged. But nothing in human culture that honored or glorified God will be lost. The best of human civilization on this fallen planet gives us a glimpse of what's ahead when the world is renewed.

The new earth will be filled with the sum total and best of purified, God-glorifying cultural expressions. But that's only the beginning. Earlier in the chapter, I cited Daniel's prophecy that in God's kingdom on earth *"the **dominion** and the **greatness** of the kingdom under the whole heavens shall be given to the people of the saints of the Most High"* (Daniel 7:27, AMP). *Greatness* comes from a root word meaning "increase" (Strong 2004). Can you imagine what men and women will produce when we have been fully perfected and our motive in everything is to glorify and honor God?

TOO GOOD TO BE TRUE?

Once again, these descriptions of the life to come may sound too unspiritual to be accurate. Permit me to make three points.

One: It's Part of Our Purpose

God created human beings to live and reign on this earth. The Bible begins with the Lord giving men rulership in the earth and it ends with men reigning on earth. *"And they* [God's sons and daughters] *shall reign for ever and ever"* (Revelation 22:5, KJV). Almighty God intended humanity to be more than caretakers of the planet. Angels could have fulfilled that role. The Lord purposed that we would create and shape earth's culture.

I mentioned earlier that John saw people in the invisible realm waiting to return to earth to *reign*. This word carries the idea of "reigning with Christ and enjoying the privileges, honors, blessings, and happiness of His kingdom" (Strong 2004). God's redeemed men and women in the present Heaven are anticipating coming back to earth to fulfill their created purpose. They expect to live physical lives in a material world—lives that fully glorify the Lord as they utilize and enjoy the beauty, blessings, benefits, and provisions of the home He created for His family.

We know that people retain memories and knowledge after they leave this life. Therefore, when those in Heaven return to earth, they will remember how they lived and what was learned and discovered during their lifetimes. And even if the Lord's redeemed family has to start from scratch on the new earth, within a very short time, civilization will be up and running again.

Two: God Has Equipped Us to Do It

The creativity and inventiveness that produce culture aren't inherently evil. They're part of the image of God that men and women bear even in our fallen condition. When the Lord God commanded Moses and the Hebrew people to construct the first Tabernacle, He gave certain individuals the ability to make it a work of art with designs, colors, and textures. And He gifted them with the ability to train others to do what they did. These craftsmen and artists are the first people described in the Scripture as being filled with the Holy Spirit.

> *"Look, I have chosen Bezalel...**I have filled him with the Spirit of God**, giving him great wisdom, intelligence, and skill in all kinds of crafts. He is able to*

create beautiful objects from gold, silver, and bronze. He is skilled in cutting and setting gemstones and in carving wood. Yes, he is a master at every craft" (Exodus 31:1-5, NLT).

"And the Lord has given [both Bezalel] *and Oholiab... the ability to teach their skills to others.* **The Lord has given them special skills** *as jewelers, designers, weavers, and embroiderers in blue, purple, and scarlet yarn on fine linen cloth. They excel in all the crafts needed for the work"* (Exodus 35:34-35, NLT).

Remember Solomon, the great king of Israel? God-given wisdom resulted in tremendous curiosity and creativity, which he employed to glorify the Lord.

*"**God gave Solomon great wisdom and understanding, and knowledge too vast to be measured**... He composed some 3,000 proverbs and wrote 1,005 songs. He could speak with authority about all kinds of plants, from the great cedar of Lebanon to the tiny hyssop that grows from cracks in a wall. He could also speak about animals, birds, reptiles, and fish. And kings from every nation sent their ambassadors to listen to the wisdom of Solomon"* (1 Kings 4:29-34, NLT).

"When the queen of Sheba heard of Solomon's reputation [for wisdom], *which brought honor to the name of the Lord, she came to test him with hard questions"* (1 Kings 10:1, NLT).

Three: It Glorifies God

People tend to think that only church-related activities can glorify God. But any righteous or right action we take using our God-given talents reflects back to Him. When you bake a cake, raise a crop, write a book, or build a table, you exercise your God-given creativity and fulfill His first command to subdue the earth by using its resources. If your motive is to honor the Lord and bless others, then your effort is a God-glorifying expression.

> *"In the same way, let your good deeds shine out for all to see, so that everyone will praise your heavenly Father"* (Matthew 5:16, NLT).

> *"So then, whether you eat or drink, or whatever you may do, do all for the honor and glory of God"* (1 Corinthians 10:31, AMP).

THE SPLENDOR OF THE KINGDOMS

In his vision of the new earth, John observed kings coming to the capital city. These rulers were bringing cultural output from their various people groups. *"And the rulers and leaders of the earth shall bring into* [the city]...***the glory— the splendor and majesty—and the honor of the nations"*** (Revelation 21:24-26, AMP). The grandeur and glory of a great civilization encompasses more than the power and authority it wields. Its distinctiveness includes cultural expressions.

John's description of these gift-bearing rulers is actually the fulfillment of a scene first described by Isaiah when he wrote a detailed passage about life on the new earth. Isaiah's prophecy reveals that these kings will bring the yield of their nations to

New Jerusalem.

> *"Nations will come to your light, and kings to the brightness of your dawn...the wealth on the seas will be brought to you...the riches of the nations will come. Herds of camels will cover your land, young camels of Midian and Ephah. And all from Sheba will come, bearing gold and incense...all Kedar's flocks will be gathered to you, the rams of Nebaioth will serve you"* (Isaiah 60:3-7, NIV).

Notice that the items being brought to the city of the Great King are familiar cultural products. This is more evidence that what's ahead on the new earth will be life as we've known it—cleansed but familiar, new but recognizable.

› →›››› • ‹‹‹‹← ‹

In the beginning, God gave men and women dominion and commissioned them to use their God-given creativity, gifts, and talents to produce God-glorifying cultures and civilizations. Sin temporarily thwarted the plan, but this purpose will be fully realized on the new earth.

Jesus redeemed us to restore us to our created purpose: sonship and dominion. We'll forever reign on earth as we subdue it, utilizing its vast resources to produce ways of life that glorify the Lord and bless men.

LIFE ON THE NEW EARTH

God's purpose in redemption isn't to replace what He created with something else. He intends to restore both His family and the home He made for us to what He planned from the beginning. This includes purifying already existing cultures and civilizations. Consequently, much of life on the new earth will be familiar to us because many aspects of life as we know it will carry on.

FOOD AND CLOTHING ON THE NEW EARTH

Men and women in the present invisible Heaven eat, drink, and wear clothes. It makes no sense that we'll abandon these practices once we are reunited with our bodies, especially since both involve fulfilling God's original mandate to subdue the earth. The Lord's first instruction to Adam and Eve after He gave them dominion was to use earth's bounty for food (Genesis 1:29). And our first parents were naked in the Garden, not because the Lord is opposed to clothing, but because He wanted them to express their God-given creativity and utilize earth's raw materials to develop suitable attire.

What Will We Eat?

It's reasonable to assume that we'll enjoy many of the foods we eat now since we'll remember how to produce and prepare favorite dishes and beverages. Perhaps one of your ancestors will recreate for you a dish popular during his or her lifetime. Maybe a new friend from a foreign country will cook a meal commonly eaten in the land of his birth. There's no doubt that men and women are going to develop new, delicious food and drink from earth's plenteous resources.

Will we eat meat? Not as we know it. Obtaining meat requires the death of an animal, and there will be no death in the life to come. *"The last enemy to be destroyed is death"* (1 Corinthians 15:26, NIV). That being said, the eating of meat and the enjoyment it brings has been and is part of many cultures. The thought of never having another steak, piece of fish, or leg of lamb makes the life ahead seem like loss rather than gain. Surely the Lord can provide—or God-given human creativity will devise—a delicious meat substitute that doesn't involve killing a creature. The new earth will have more, not less, resources.

What Will We Wear?

Clothing reflects nationality and individuality. Because both continue in the life to come, it's likely that clothing on the new earth will express those traits as people wear what's normal for them. Normal is going to vary from culture to culture and individual to individual, as it does now. Robes were normal in Bible days. Those people may choose to wear robes on the new earth. Perhaps some of us will decide we like them as well. Maybe some first-century folks will choose blue jeans for everyday wear. As I explained in Chapter 4, it's also reasonable to presume that just as we have certain outfits for specific occasions now, that's how it will be on the new earth.

Obviously, attire that is immodest or worn for vanity won't have any place in our future home. But God certainly isn't opposed to colorful or distinctive clothing. The prophet Ezekiel was sent to Israel at a time when they had abandoned the Lord to worship idols. God, through the prophet, endeavored to call His people back to Him by reminding them of what He had done for them in the past. The Lord said, *"I made a covenant with you...and you became mine"* (Ezekiel 16:8, NLT). Then He described how He adorned Israel after they were joined to Him through this solemn agreement.

> *"I **gave you expensive clothing of linen and silk, beautifully embroidered**, and **sandals made of fine leather**. I gave you **lovely jewelry, bracelets, and beautiful necklaces**, a **ring** for your nose and **earrings** for your ears, and a **lovely crown** for your head. And so you were made beautiful with **gold** and **silver**. Your **clothes** were made of **fine linen** and were **beautifully embroidered**"* (Ezekiel 16:10-13, NLT).

There's a lot of symbolism in this statement, but note one point: this is the Lord's own description of His actions. Beautiful, colorful clothing, jewelry, and shoes can't be wicked or inappropriate since Almighty God uses it as an example of how He adorns His people. Consider what the Lord God told Moses when He informed him that he'd be used to lead Israel out of slavery in Egypt:

> *"And I will see to it that the Egyptians treat you well. They will load you down with gifts so you will not leave empty-handed. The Israelite women will ask for*

silver and gold jewelry and fine clothing from their Egyptian neighbors and their neighbors' guests. With this clothing, you will dress your sons and daughters. In this way, you will plunder the Egyptians" (Exodus 3:21-22, NLT).

Israel's deliverance from bondage is called redemption (Exodus 6:6). Although it was a real event that actually happened, their deliverance also pictures the redemption Jesus Christ provided for us through the Cross. Notice that clothing was delivered out of Egypt along with the people. Why would the Bible include this detail if clothes aren't part of the plan for God's family? Clothing is going to be redeemed along with the rest of mankind's cultural output.

WORK ON THE NEW EARTH

The Lord created human beings with the desire and capacity to engage in meaningful, satisfying work. That's hard to envision since work is tiresome and unsatisfying for many in this life. Work was never supposed to be this way and only became so when Adam disobeyed God (Genesis 3:17-19). But in the life ahead, tedious and unfruitful labor will disappear. On the new earth, men and women are going to engage in activities that are meaningful, not wearisome, amid the beauty of God's creation in perfect fellowship with Him. Everything we do will be pleasing to the Lord and fulfilling for us.

As we discovered in the previous chapter, God invested human beings with passion, creativity, and inventiveness and then commissioned us to use those abilities to subdue the earth. Subduing the earth involves controlling its resources and processes. This means finding out where various raw materials are located and learning how to turn them into finished products.

It requires observing and understanding planting and harvesting cycles as well as uncovering natural forces like electricity and natural laws, such as the law of gravity. Down through the centuries, these endeavors have given rise to many industries and technologies:

- Studying and researching the earth in order to discover and understand its processes (science).

- Developing the means of production needed to utilize earth's resources (industry, engineering, agriculture, animal husbandry, metallurgy).

- Bringing about related activities along with procedures to deliver products and information to others (transportation, shipping, commerce, business, writing, paper, books).

Human beings have engaged in varying degrees of all these operations since the beginning of time. In keeping with the principle of continuity, we can expect these activities to be present on the new earth, cleansed of the corruption that makes them laborious. I realize it's difficult to picture these pursuits as sources of fulfillment since we've only known the drudgery of life in a sin damaged world. But on the new earth, men and women are going to pursue these employments out of desire based on their God-given giftings and talents, not out of necessity.

You may have had an interest in marine biology but couldn't afford a college education and ended up working a job you don't really like. When the world is made new, you'll have the resources and time to pursue your dream and fulfill your passion in a way that's entirely glorifying to the Lord. Imagine having the freedom and ability to engage in pursuits unavailable to you in this life.

WHAT KINDS OF THINGS WILL WE DO?

The Bible actually refers to a variety of specific jobs on the new earth. God's Word tells us men and women will build homes and farm the land (Isaiah 65:21). This suggests that, in addition to building and planting, some are going to be involved in the production and assembly of related materials.

- House construction requires lumber, bricks, mortar, nails, pipes, wires, shingles, glass, and a multitude of other items. Decorative articles and furnishing that make a house a comfortable home are also needed.

- Farming requires assembling and producing items, such as seed, tractors, and threshers, along with the objects essential to storing, distributing, preparing, and consuming the crops produced.

We know from the Bible that there will be nations with rulers. This means systems of government with people working in administrative capacities. In the context of the kingdom of God coming to earth, Jesus said that some of His faithful followers are going to be rewarded with administrative positions. *"You are a trustworthy servant. You have been faithful with the little I entrusted to you, so you will be governor of ten cities as your reward... [and to another] you can be governor over five cities"* (Luke 19:17-18, NLT).

People are going to travel in the new world. The prophet Isaiah wrote about merchants in ships and caravans bringing vast wealth to the city of the Great King. The apostle John, in his vision of the world to come, saw kings of nations journeying to New Jerusalem (Isaiah 60:5-9; Revelation 21:24). And men and women will finally have the time and resources to travel and enjoy the beauties of this magnificent planet.

- Some individuals might choose to work in industries connected with these movements of people. Some may opt to provide inns, hotels, resorts, and restaurants for travelers, while others are employed in industries that produce the various modes of transportation used to move people from place to place.

- Scripture says there will be ships on the new earth. Why not cars and airplanes as well? Because of the continuation of culture, we should expect them. John reported streets in the capital city, suggesting a place for vehicles (Revelation 21:21; Revelation 22:2).

Business and Industry

Some of you may be wondering, "Why would we need businesses and industries with goods and services once earth is made new?" Technically, we won't need homes, food, or drink, but we'll have them all to enjoy. Business in and of itself isn't sinful. It comes out of regular human interaction. I have a product you require but can't provide, so I make it. I have an idea and create an object you want or need. You're more skilled at a task than I am, so you do it. Remember, we won't all be the same in the life to come. We'll retain our unique personalities, interests, and abilities. Even in this sin cursed earth, many are in business for reasons other than making a living. Their job is their passion. They want to help and bless others or make society a better place. For example, individuals often open restaurants because they love to prepare food and serve people.

Technology isn't evil. Creating and developing tools and machines of some sort exists in every culture. It's another way we exercise dominion over earth's resources. God's Word refers to many examples of both machinery and production systems (e.g., threshing floors, millstones, pottery wheels, winepresses, harnesses, yokes, and plows). These are all technological developments appropriate for the time period in which specific Bible passages were written. If Isaiah or John were recording the Scripture today, they would make reference to automated production lines, computer technologies, and delivery trucks.

The point is that life in our forever home won't be something foreign or unknown to us. We will engage in familiar pursuits and occupations. The Lord's goal in redemption isn't to replace humanity and the cultures we've produced, but to redeem us and them so that we glorify Him and bless each other.

Even with our fallen natures, we have extended our dominion to the sky, the sea, and outer space. We can fly through the air, cross the ocean above or below the water, and travel to the moon. Through automation, we've reduced the labor and time involved in performing numerous tasks. The advent of computers has changed the way we create, store, and disseminate information, connecting the world in ways undreamed of in times past. If we have accomplished these feats in a damaged world, just think of the products and technology we'll develop and produce once we're fully perfected. As we explore, utilize, and enjoy God's creation, we'll employ purified technologies from the old earth and invent new technologies presently beyond our imagination.

Science and Technology

Almighty God designed a world with wonders to be discovered and processes to be understood. The stars are an example. The Lord put them in place when He created the heavens and the earth. Since antiquity, men have used these lights in the sky to mark time and determine directions for navigational purposes. The vast, starlit expanse above has also inspired countless generations to contemplate the glory of God.

> *"The heavens declare the glory of God, and the* [sky] *shows and proclaims His handiwork"* (Psalm 19:1, AMP).

> *"When I view and consider Your heavens, the work of Your fingers, the moon and the stars which You have ordained and established; What is man, that You are mindful of him, and...care for him?"* (Psalm 8:3-4, AMP).

Ancient people saw only a fraction of the stars. But they were all there, waiting to be discovered in the ages to come as men advanced in technology and science. Those advancements led mankind to venture into outer space in the twentieth century. That's only the beginning because God created billions of galaxies. In the life to come, we'll use our God-given creativity and inventiveness and find new ways to search out the marvels of His creation. We'll have an eternity to discover increasing aspects of the heavens and the earth as they disclose ever more of the majesty and beauty of the One who created it all.

LIFE WITH NO CHALLENGES?

I've had more than one person tell me they're concerned that the life to come is going to be boring because there will be nothing to do. Hopefully, you're starting to realize this won't be the case since God's goal in redemption is to restore what He originally planned. His first charge to humanity before sin entered the picture was: *"Fill the earth...and bring it under your control"* (Genesis 1:28, CEV). His commission required human beings to deal with challenges as they discovered earth's resources and identified its processes and principles. The Lord knew there would be problems to solve and obstacles to overcome, so He equipped humanity to accomplish these tasks by giving us intellect and curiosity and designing us to investigate, discover, and accomplish. We're made to face, overcome, and enjoy challenges. Striving for and reaching goals is in our DNA.

These God-given traits won't vanish in the life ahead. Just the opposite—they'll be fully employed. We'll continue to fulfill our dominion mandate once earth is made new. But our efforts will no longer be toilsome. They'll be fruitful and satisfying, unmarred by the frustrations and struggles of life in a sin damaged world. When one challenge is met, we'll look forward to another. When one adventure has ended, we'll anticipate the next. Part of the joy of living is the anticipation of what's ahead. That's the way God made us.

Maybe you're thinking, "Won't we run out of things to do?" No, because God's kingdom on earth is going to last forever and increase. In one of the greatest prophecies about the coming Redeemer, Jesus, the prophet Isaiah wrote:

> *"For unto us a child is born, unto us a son is given: and the government shall be upon his shoulder: and his name shall be called Wonderful, Counsellor, The mighty God, The everlasting Father, The Prince of Peace. Of the **increase** of his government and peace there shall be no end"* (Isaiah 9:6-7, KJV).

In the original Hebrew language, *increase* means "expansion"

(Strong 2004): *"Power and peace will be in his kingdom and will continue to grow forever"* (Isaiah 9:7, NCV). The Lord's governance of the new heavens and new earth will be ever expanding: *"Ever wider shall his dominion spread, endlessly at peace"* (Isaiah 9:7, The Word [Knox], p. 1321). What an intriguing statement! Is the Lord going to create new worlds? Will the universe—with its countless galaxies and millions and billions of stars and, no telling how many, planets—turn out to be so vast that it takes eons to explore and subdue? Is it going to continue to expand forever?

We'll have to wait and see exactly what Isaiah's prophecy means. But it's certain we'll never run out of things to do or places to go. Nor will we exhaust the challenges and opportunities in the life to come. And as we carry out our mandate to subdue the earth, we'll learn more and more about its processes and the wonders of God's creation.

, →**]]]** · **[[[**← ·

Life on the new earth won't be foreign; it will be familiar. Just like the landscapes around us, the way we live will be changed but recognizable. We'll build homes, prepare food, fashion clothing, and work at meaningful, satisfying endeavors as we fulfill God's command to subdue the earth. But that's not all we'll do. Many other activities common to human culture will be present on the new earth. In the next chapter, we'll take a look at some of them.

MORE ABOUT LIFE
ON THE NEW EARTH

One of the most frequent concerns I hear people voice when they admit their hesitancies about Heaven is the fear that it won't be much fun. All of us have interests and enjoy activities that, although not sinful, don't seem spiritual enough for Heaven—like reading a riveting book, watching an exciting movie, attending a concert, going on a hike, playing a game, cheering our favorite sports team, or pursuing a hobby. Will there be any such amusements in the life to come? According to the Bible, the answer is yes!

THE JOY OF REST AND RECREATION

Scripture states that when God completed His work of creation, He rested: *"By the seventh day God had finished the work he had been doing; so on the seventh day he rested from all his work"* (Genesis 2:2, NIV). Almighty God didn't need to rest because He was tired. Instead, the Lord set aside time to take satisfaction in His completed work. He not only observed all He created and declared it to be exceedingly good, He rejoiced over His works (Genesis 1:31; Psalm 104:31).

Adam and Eve lived in Eden at the time and participated in the rest of God. They joined with the Lord God, delighting in the beauty and bounty of the home He made for them. Unfortunately, when our first parents sinned, mankind lost the blessing of sharing in God's rest. Nonetheless, the concept of setting aside time to rest was planted in mankind's consciousness.

- Since the earliest ages of man on earth, every known culture has made time for leisure or freedom from work-related endeavors. And in those times, they engaged in recreational activities.

- This won't change on the new earth. Yes, we will work, but we'll also play. If this thought shocks you, keep in mind that the life to come will be new but recognizable, changed but familiar. Remember, God's purpose in redemption is to restore what was lost to sin.

As the Lord began to unveil His plan of redemption through His prophets, He instructed His people to observe a day of rest called a Sabbath. This day pictured the rest that the Redeemer will provide on the new earth—a restoration of unbroken fellowship with God as we enjoy the blessings of our amazing forever home. The Greek word used for the rest of God and His people carries the idea of "refreshment" (Strong 2004).

Possibly you're thinking, "Why will we need leisure time and amusements if work is finally going to be enjoyable? Why would we need rest and refreshment if we have immortal, incorruptible, resurrected bodies?" As we learned in previous chapters, life in a perfect world won't be without challenges, and we'll still be finite people. We will likely welcome a rest after expending energy to accomplish a challenging task. Rest isn't sinful. Like our first parents before they sinned, after working hard, we'll be able to experience the joy of relaxation in a world free from corruption and death.

And in these times of rest and recreation, we'll have plenty to entertain us beginning with the magnificence of creation itself. Earth's wonders aren't simply useful, they're a source of pleasure. Trees not only yield wood, they give enjoyment through their beauty and majesty, their shade and fruit. The Lord Himself delights in His creation and, as beings made in His image, so do we.

> *"May the glory of the Lord be forever. May the Lord enjoy what he has made"* (Psalm 104:31, NCV). *"The highest heavens belong to the Lord, but the earth he has given to man"* (Psalm 115:16, NIV).

Currently, Almighty God is the only one who sees most of this world's beauty. He sees flowers in secluded alpine valleys, tree frogs deep in remote jungles, spectacular plant life and colorful creatures in the depths of the sea, and fantastic rock formations in isolated canyons. But this is going to change in the life ahead because we'll have the time and resources to travel and enjoy the natural wonders of this planet.

What else will we do with our leisure time? All cultures on earth, going back to the earliest generations of humankind, have produced various forms of amusement ranging from very primitive to highly sophisticated art, music, dancing, storytelling, and athletic competitions. Based on the principle of continuity, these types of entertainment will be present on the new earth, delivered from the effects of sin. They will be fully glorifying to the Lord and completely satisfying to His family.

ART

God is the Master Artist. His creation overflows with colors, textures, shapes, and designs from the tiniest bits of moss growing on rocks to the majestic expanses of plains, seas, and mountains. He has decorated His world with vibrant birds and brilliant flowers. Therefore, it's not surprising that His image bearers do the same. Since the dawn of time, human beings have produced works of art, whether a design carved in a tree trunk or a symbol painted on a rock. As technology advanced, so did mankind's means and methods of artistic expression.

Unhappily, down through the centuries, much of humanity's artwork has failed to glorify the Lord. But it will be different on the new earth. Human creativity and artistic expression will reach its full potential as men and women carry out God's command to subdue the earth. Artists are going to utilize earth's raw materials to paint, carve, and sculpt as all of their works bring honor to the One who inspired and gifted them.

Maybe you have a natural talent for drawing and longed to go to art school, but life took you a different direction. Perhaps you always wanted to learn to paint or sculpt but never had the time or resources. In the life ahead, you will put these unused gifts and talents to work and realize your dream as your creative ability is fully expressed.

MUSIC AND DANCING

Although singing, dancing, and musical instruments have been used for wicked purposes in this fallen world, in the life after this life, they'll be purified. This may be surprising if you come from a stream of Christianity that believes music and dancing are sinful. But in the parable of the prodigal son, Jesus implied that these activities take place in Heaven (Luke 15:11). Jesus told this story to illustrate Heaven's response when lost sinners come back to God. He described a joyful celebration with feasting, music, and dancing (Luke 15:22-25). Our Savior would not have included such details if any of these amusements are inherently evil or if they're not part of the life ahead.

Music in Heaven

The Bible reveals that there's music in the present Heaven. The apostle John reported that he heard singing and saw musical instruments in the unseen realm.

- *"And as he* [Jesus] *took the scroll...Each one* [beings and people around the throne of God] *had a **harp**...And they **sang** a new **song** with these words"* (Revelation 5:8-9, NLT).

- *"And I saw the seven angels who stand before God, and they were given seven **trumpets**...Then the seven angels with the seven **trumpets** prepared to blow their mighty blasts"* (Revelation 8:2-6, NLT). Although these particular horns weren't blown for entertainment but to announce events about to transpire on earth, their presence in Heaven reveals that such instruments can be glorifying to Almighty God.

Music comes from God. He's the One who fashioned men and women with the capacity to create and use musical instruments, compose and sing songs, and dance exuberantly before Him. Scripture is filled with examples of people joyfully praising the Lord through song and dance and skillfully played instruments.

149

- In the Book of Psalms, God's people are instructed to praise Him with songs and instruments. *"Praise the Lord... Praise him with a blast of the **trumpet**; praise him with the **lyre** and **harp**! Praise him with the **tambourine** and **dancing**; praise him with **stringed instruments** and **flutes**! Praise him **with** a clash of **cymbals**; praise him with **loud clanging cymbals**. Let everything that lives **sing praises** to the Lord"* (Psalm 150:1-6, NLT).

- When Israel was safely through the parted Red Sea after escaping bondage in Egypt, they held a joyous celebration. *"Then Moses and the people of Israel **sang** this **song** to the Lord. Then Miriam the prophet, Aaron's sister, took a **tambourine** and led all the women in **rhythm** and **dancing**"* (Exodus 15:1; Exodus 15:20, NLT).

Music will be redeemed. Part of God's promise to His people includes restoration of joyful singing and dancing. *"I will rebuild you, [My people]. You will again be happy and **dance merrily with tambourines**"* (Jeremiah 31:4, NLT).

- Referring to the new earth, the prophet Isaiah wrote, *"The Lord will comfort Israel again and make her deserts blossom. Her barren wilderness will become as beautiful as Eden—the garden of the LORD. Joy and gladness will be found there. **Lovely songs of thanksgiving** will fill the air"* (Isaiah 51:3, NLT).

- The Lord Himself is going to sing. *"For the LORD your God has arrived to live among you. He is a mighty savior. He will rejoice over you with great gladness. With his love, he will calm all your fears. He will exult over you **by singing a happy song**"* (Zephaniah 3:17, NLT).

One of the themes we've emphasized thus far is cultural continuity. John noted an intriguing detail regarding continuation of activities from this life to the next when he described his time in Heaven. He wrote that he saw men and women who *"were all holding harps that God had given them. And they were **singing the song of Moses**, the servant of God, and the song of the Lamb"* (Revelation 15:2-3, NLT).

- Moses composed several songs during his lifetime that are recorded in the Bible (Exodus 15:1-18; Deuteronomy 32:1-43). It's not clear whether the people John observed were singing one of those songs or a new song written by Moses since he's been in Heaven.

- Either way, this detail indicates things that glorified God in this life, such as Moses' songs, won't be lost, and the life to come won't mean the end of human creativity and musical expression.

What About Electric Guitars?

Perhaps you're wondering about instruments other than those mentioned in the verses we've cited, those invented since Bible days, such as tubas, violins, pianos, and electric guitars. Will they be used on the new earth? It's likely. The development and production of musical instruments is an example of human beings using God-given creativity to transform natural resources into items that glorify the Lord and bless people—a purpose we'll carry on forever.

I've had people ask me what type of music is played in Heaven. The Bible doesn't address this issue, but keep these thoughts in mind:

- Since cultural identity survives, we can presume we'll play and listen to what we enjoyed on earth. Throughout history, many songs and musical works have been composed for the glory of God. Of course, nothing sinful will be retained.

- Since personal identity continues past this life, we'll have varying tastes in music, as we do now. People who lived in Western Europe during the Medieval Period may prefer a Gregorian chant to the more contemporary styles familiar to us. Our musical preferences will likely expand as we're exposed to music types from other cultures and time periods. And we'll appreciate the praise and honor they bring to the Lord even if a particular genre doesn't become our favorite.

We can't yet answer every question about what's ahead. But we know that it's gain, not loss. You may have desired to play the piano or guitar but, due to the circumstances of life, never had the opportunity to learn. Your dream will be fulfilled on the new earth. Personally, I have loved ballet since I was a child. It is such a beautiful way to express grace and joy. My life didn't go that way, and I'm much too old to take up ballet now. But I look forward to realizing this desire in our forever home.

STORYTELLING

The telling of interesting, intriguing, and amusing stories dates back to mankind's earliest days on the planet. Everyone enjoys a great story, whether it's a dramatic account of good triumphing over evil, a humorous tale that makes us laugh, or a mystery that keeps us guessing until the end. Humanity's love for this universal form of entertainment won't cease in the life to come.

- Jesus made a number of references to people sitting around tables to eat and fellowship in Heaven: *"And I tell you this, that many...will come from all over the world and sit down with Abraham, Isaac, and Jacob at the feast in the Kingdom of Heaven"* (Matthew 8:11, NLT). People laugh and tell stories in this kind of setting.

- The Lord Jesus was an outstanding storyteller. He regularly used parables or short stories to convey wisdom and spiritual truths. If it was appropriate for our Savior to tell stories, so it will be for the rest of God's family in Heaven and on the new earth.

Our appreciation for inspiring and entertaining stories isn't wrong. Almighty God made us this way. It's part of His image in us. The greatest story ever told was authored and directed by our Creator—His own saga of redemption. As the Lord worked out this plan to deliver His creation from bondage to sin, corruption, and death, He inspired men to write a record of the unfolding drama—the Bible. God's book tells the story of His desire for a family and the lengths He's gone to in obtaining it. His instruction to His people through the centuries has always been to tell the story of what He's done.

- *"O my people, listen to my teaching. Open your ears to what I am saying, for I will speak to you in a parable. I will teach you hidden lessons from our past—stories we have heard and know, stories our ancestors handed down to us"* (Psalm 78:1-3, NLT).

- *"We will not hide these truths from our children but will tell the next generation about the glorious deeds of the Lord. We will tell of his power and the mighty miracles he did"* (Psalm 78:4, NLT).

Books in Heaven and on the New Earth

Every culture on earth that developed writing has also produced written records of their stories. Thus, because of the continuance of culture, we can assume there will be books on the new earth. We know for certain there are books in the invisible Heaven.

- The psalmist David wrote: *"You* [God] *saw me before I was born. Every day of my life was recorded in your book…You keep track of all my sorrows. You have collected all my tears in your bottle. You have recorded each one in your book"* (Psalm 139:16; Psalm 56:8, NLT).

- John reported seeing books in Heaven. *"And I saw a scroll* [book]*, in the right hand of the one who was sitting on the throne…I saw another mighty angel coming down from heaven…And in his hand was a small scroll* [book] *which he unrolled…And the books were opened, including the Book of Life. And the dead were judged according to the things written in the books"* (Revelation 5:1; Revelation 10:1-2; Revelation 20:12, NLT).

Are there other books besides God's in the unseen world? No doubt. Keep in mind, nothing that glorifies the Lord will be lost. Through the centuries, many great literary works have been written for His glory, including prose, poetry, and plays. Remember that the creative ability to pen these works comes from Him. Such books will be redeemed and survive to Heaven and the new earth. And new books are going to be written. There will be more information available, and people will have the passion, curiosity, and creativity to write without the roadblocks and time constraints that hinder us in this fallen world.

Some may ask, "Won't the stories that survive to the new earth need to be made pristine (a code word for boring)?" Certainly, nothing impure will make it to the life ahead. But God's own book, the Bible, portrays murder, intrigue, betrayal, and adultery, not for the sake of exalting evil, but to magnify the Lord by showing how His love and grace triumphs in and over the darkest of behaviors and circumstances.

What About Movies and TV?

As mankind's technological developments have advanced so have the methods by which stories are conveyed. We've gone from memorizing stories and passing them along orally around campfires to handwritten scrolls and then to printed volumes. Human creativity has taken storytelling even further in the last one hundred years with movies, radio, and television. Now we have DVDs, MP3 players, smartphones, e-books, and YouTube™. Yes, these venues have been used by sinful people as a means of spreading wickedness. But like other cultural output, they'll be purified. And we can expect new technology to be developed.

SPORTS

We should also anticipate athletic activities in our future home. If the thought of people playing a round of golf or cheering for a soccer team on the new earth seems absurd, think about this:

- God made us in such a way that we enjoy exhilarating experiences. Our bodies are fashioned to run, jump, and throw. We're suited for sports.

- Every culture engages in skilled physical competition

of some sort, be it a foot race down a jungle path or an elaborate sports spectacle in a crowded arena. This won't change when the world is made new. It's part of cultural continuity.

- Athletic pursuits not only provide enjoyment but also offer opportunities to fulfill God's command to subdue the earth. When we climb a cliff, ski down a snow-covered slope, or swim across a lake, we utilize equipment crafted from earth's bounty and demonstrate our dominion over certain natural laws. Riding a bike not only requires using natural resources to make the bicycle but also reigning over gravity through balancing on two wheels.

You may question whether or not athletic competitions are even possible on the new earth. Can someone lose a game or come in second in a perfect world? Of course! Don't forget what was covered earlier in the book: we won't all be the same in the life to come. We will retain our individuality and uniqueness. Just as some of us now have more athletic ability and others less, that's how it will be in the new world. If you never kicked a soccer ball before in your life, you won't suddenly become an all-star player. You won't morph into an Olympic gold medalist if you've never run a lap around a track. And, as finite beings, just as we'll be able to grow in knowledge in the life to come, we'll be capable of developing greater skills.

There's nothing sinful about competition between people of varying skill levels. Granted, competition between fallen people can and does produce sin in this life. But the Bible compares Christian life to athletic competitions. If such activity is intrinsically evil, why would the Holy Spirit make such a comparison?

"Therefore, since we are surrounded by such a great cloud of witnesses, let us throw off everything that hinders and the sin that so easily entangles, and let us run with perseverance the race marked out for us" (Hebrews 12:1, NIV).

"Do you not know that in a race all the runners run, but only one gets the prize? Run in such a way as to get the prize. Everyone who competes in the games goes into strict training. They do it to get a crown that will not last; but we do it to get a crown that will last forever" (1 Corinthians 9:24-25, NIV).

Even in this sin damaged world, gifted athletes use their God-given talents and abilities to honor the Lord. Think of some of the well-known, committed Christian athletes in professional sports in recent years. They openly acknowledge Almighty God as they humbly thank Him for their successes and use their fame and fortune to help their fellow man.

I'll address this more fully in the last chapter, but part of the gain of the life to come is the realization of unfulfilled dreams and desires. How many people dreamed of playing a particular sport, but life's challenges got in the way and it never happened? That's not the end of their story, though. They'll achieve those aspirations on the new earth.

, ⟶⟩⟩⟩⟩ · ⟨⟨⟨⟨⟵ ·

The Lord's purposes for mankind and the earth will be realized. His home will be our home and all that we do—whether at work or play—will glorify Him and fulfill us. Our surroundings are going to feel like home and life will be familiar. Life at its best now gives us a glimpse of what's ahead on the new earth.

ANIMALS IN HEAVEN

Before moving on, I need to address a vitally important topic—animals in Heaven. If you're not an animal lover, you may disagree with an entire chapter devoted to their ultimate fate. However, this is a critical issue for those of us who have experienced the death of a beloved pet. Even if you're not a fan of cats and dogs, their destiny still involves you because our future is linked with theirs. Greater understanding of what's ahead for the creatures of earth gives us insight into what awaits us.

THE PLACE OF ANIMALS

Let's begin by considering the place of animals in creation. They're earth's second most important inhabitants behind man. Almighty God created them to benefit us. Among other things, they provide a level of companionship. The Bible refers to God's creation of animals in the context of man's relational needs.

> *"And the LORD God said, 'It is not good for the man to be alone. I will make a companion who will help him.' So the LORD God formed from the soil every*

kind of animal and bird. He brought them to Adam to see what he would call them, and Adam chose a name for each one. He gave names to all the livestock, birds, and wild animals. But still there was no companion suitable for him" (Genesis 2:18-20, NLT).

Although these creatures partially fulfilled Adam's need for companionship, the Lord had more in mind for him. God intended to create a suitable companion for Adam, or one like Adam, which is how the passage reads in the original Hebrew language. Adam found that relationship with Eve, whom God formed from a rib taken out of the man's side. Even though animals weren't the ultimate in companionship, a connection was made between us and them when God brought His creatures to Adam and instructed him to name them. Deciding on and giving names establishes relationship. The Lord God gave Adam the privilege of naming Eve as well (Genesis 3:20).

God Cares for and Enjoys Animals

According to the Lord Jesus, although men have more value than animals, animals matter to God. When Jesus exhorted His followers not to worry about having life's necessities, He referred to His Father's care of birds and flowers.

"Look at the birds. They don't need to plant or harvest or put food in barns because your heavenly Father feeds them. And you are far more valuable to him than they are" (Matthew 6:26, NLT).

Numerous Bible passages assure us that the Lord cares for the creatures of earth. *"The Lord is good to all, and His tender mercies are over all His works—**the entirety of things created**"* (Psalm 145:9, AMP). *"**All living things look to you** for food,*

160

*and you give it to them at the right time. You open your hand, and **you satisfy all living things** "* (Psalm 145:15-16, NCV). *"O Lord, **you preserve both man and beast** "* (Psalm 36:6, NIV).

Not only does Almighty God care for animals but He takes pleasure in them. The Bible says that *"[He] rejoices in all he has made"* (Psalm 104:31, NLT). Keep in mind that God is the only one who sees most of the creatures of earth—those hidden within the dense forests, thick jungles, and deep seas. The Bible further reveals that the Lord gave His creatures the capacity to enjoy their surroundings, and He delights in watching them play.

> *"There is the sea, vast and spacious, teeming with creatures beyond number—living things both large and small. There the ships go to and fro, and the leviathan* [a large sea animal], *which you formed to frolic there"* (Psalm 104:25-26, NIV).

- The root word translated *frolic* means "to laugh in pleasure (and) by implication, to play" (Strong 2004). God fashioned these creatures to play. That's more than mere existence. It's quality of life.

- The Jerusalem Bible phrases it this way: *"Leviathan whom you made to amuse you"* (Psalm 104:26, The Word [Jerusalem], p. 1108). The Lord Himself enjoys the animals He created.

MEN AND ANIMALS ARE LINKED

Creation, in its present condition, is not as God meant it to be. He didn't fashion lions to eat lambs, hawks to devour doves, or alligators to eat humans. Nor did He make trees and flowers to become diseased, wither, and die. The Lord didn't create anyone or anything to perish. The material world was subjected to death through Adam's sin. As the head of the human race and the first steward of earth, Adam's actions directly affected both the family resident in him and the home God made for us. *"When Adam sinned, sin entered the entire human race. His sin spread death throughout all the world, so everything began to grow old and die"* (Romans 5:12, TLB).

Because of Adam's disobedience, men and women, animals, plants, and the earth itself were infused with death. God's remedy for this condition is redemption through Jesus Christ. The Cross is big enough to deliver both mankind and the earth, along with its creatures, from sin and its effects.

> *"He* [Jesus] *was supreme in the beginning and—leading the resurrection parade—he is supreme in the end. From beginning to end he's there, towering far above everything, everyone. So spacious is he, so roomy, that everything of God finds its proper place in him without crowding. Not only that, but all the broken and dislocated pieces of the universe—people and things, animals and atoms—get properly fixed and fit together in vibrant harmonies, all because of his death, his blood that poured down from the Cross"* (Colossians 1:18-20, The Message).

I am in no way saying that animals are equal with human beings. They're not. Men are made in the image of God; animals aren't. Men need a Savior because of their sin; animals don't sin. Yet there's a sense in which Jesus died for the creatures of earth indirectly because His sacrifice provides deliverance or redemption for what has been damaged by sin. The Lord God won't surrender any part of the home He made for Himself and

His family to death—including the animals. The creatures of earth belong to Him.

> *"For every beast of the forest is Mine and the cattle upon a thousand hills or upon the mountains where thousands are. I know and am acquainted with all the birds of the mountains, and the wild animals of the field are Mine and are with Me, in My mind"* (Psalm 50:10-11, AMP).

Animals have been present on this planet since the beginning of time. They're part of the home the Lord God created for His family, and they won't be absent from our renewed and restored home. There will be animals on the new earth. The Old Testament prophets wrote that when the Redeemer sets up His eternal kingdom on earth and removes the curse of sin and death, animals won't harm each other or man any longer. The harmony that existed among God's creatures before sin occurred will be restored. All of creation will finally be as the Lord intended (see note 6).

> "[My people] *will no longer be prey for other nations, and wild animals will no longer attack them"* (Ezekiel 34:28, NLT).

> *"In that day the wolf and the lamb will live together; the leopard and the goat will be at peace. Calves and yearlings will be safe among lions, and a little child will lead them all. The cattle will graze among bears. Cubs and calves will lie down together. And lions will eat grass as livestock do ...Nothing will hurt or destroy in all my holy mountain"* (Isaiah 11:6-9, NLT).

Animals Will Live Again

The great apostle Paul wrote that all of creation longs to be free from bondage to corruption and death. He further revealed that the Lord will deliver His entire material creation from this condition when He raises His sons and daughters from the dead.

> *"For all creation is waiting patiently and hopefully for that future day when God will resurrect his children. For on that day thorns and thistles, sin, death, and decay...will all disappear, and the world around us will share in the glorious freedom from sin which God's children enjoy. For we know that even the things of nature, like animals and plants, suffer in sickness and death as they await this great event"* (Romans 8:19-22, TLB).

> *"And even we Christians, although we have the Holy Spirit within us as a foretaste of future glory, also groan to be released from pain and suffering. We, too, wait anxiously for that day when God will give us our full rights as his children, including the new bodies he has promised us—bodies that will never be sick again and will never die"* (Romans 8:23, TLB).

The language in this passage indicates that what happens to men and women will happen to animals. They'll be released from corruption when we are released. Not only will the Lord raise our bodies from the grave, He's going to free His original animal creation from death by raising them up as well. If this sounds too incredible to believe, look at another portion of the psalm we quoted earlier in the chapter.

"There is the sea, vast and spacious, teeming with creatures beyond number—living things both large and small. There the ships go to and fro, and the leviathan, which you formed to frolic there. These all look to you to give them their food at the proper time. When you give it to them, they gather it up; when you open your hand, they are satisfied with good things" (Psalm 104:25-28, NIV).

"When you hide your face, they are terrified; when you take away their breath, they die and return to the dust. When you send your Spirit, they are created, and you **renew** *the face of the earth"* (Psalm 104:29-30, NIV).

Notice the description given of the death of these creatures. When animals die, their bodies—like ours—return to dust. But according to the Bible, when God sends His Spirit, they are created and the face of the earth is renewed. *Renew* means "to rebuild" as opposed to making something that never existed before (Strong 2004).

Earlier in the book, I discussed how the earth is going to be renewed or restored when Almighty God establishes His visible kingdom here. Jesus' return to this world will signal *"the final recovery of all things from sin"* (Acts 3:21, TLB). God won't make an earth that never existed before. He'll make this earth new again. As part of this renewal, He'll resurrect the animals. The Lord won't create new animals. He'll make those He already created new by delivering them from slavery to corruption. He'll restore them to life on earth in a spectacular demonstration of His complete victory over death. Even species that are currently extinct are only temporarily lost.

THERE ARE ANIMALS IN HEAVEN RIGHT NOW!

We know there are animals in the present invisible Heaven because the apostle John saw them. While in the unseen realm, he observed a spectacular scene of corporate worship and animals were part of this heavenly praise service. John reported, *"I heard **every creature** in **heaven** and **on earth** and **under the earth** and **on the sea**, and all that is in them, singing: 'To him who sits on the throne and to the Lamb be praise and honor and glory and power for ever and ever'"* (Revelation 5:13, NIV).

- The word translated *creature* means "a created thing" (Strong 2004). It is used of both men and animals elsewhere in the New Testament (2 Corinthians 5:17; 1 Timothy 4:4; James 1:18).

- The only other time John used the word in recording his experience in Heaven, it means "animals" (Revelation 8:9) (Strong 2004).

As John continued to describe what he saw, the context makes it plain that both men and animals praised God: *"The four living creatures said, 'Amen,' and the* [twenty-four] *elders fell down and worshipped"* (Revelation 5:14, NIV). John mentioned these elders and living creatures seven times in the Book of Revelation. He recorded that these beings surround the throne of God and offer continuous worship. Here's his description of them:

> *"In the center, around the throne, were four living creatures, and they were covered with eyes, in front and in back. The first living creature was like a lion,*

the second was like an ox, the third had a face like a man, the fourth was like a flying eagle. Each of the four living creatures had six wings and was covered with eyes all around, even under his wings. Day and night they never stop saying: 'Holy, holy, holy is the Lord God Almighty, who was, and is, and is to come'" (Revelation 4:6-8, NIV).

The word translated *living creatures* in these passages "denotes a living being [and] animal [or beast] is the equivalent [in English]" (Vine 1984). When used in other verses in the Scripture, the word means "animals" (Hebrews 13:11; 2 Peter 2:12; Jude 10).

- John wrote that these living beings resemble a lion, an ox, a man, and an eagle. The Bible doesn't tell us exactly what they are, but they're distinct from the elders and the angels (Revelation 5:11).

- Whatever they might be, these creatures are obviously intelligent, articulate, non-human, non-angelic beings that live in Heaven and praise God. Perhaps they're prototypes or patterns of animals on earth since they bear some resemblance to animals John recognized.

John saw other animals in Heaven. He mentioned that he observed *"a solitary **eagle** flying in midheaven, and as it flew I heard it crying with a loud voice"* (Revelation 8:13, AMP). He also witnessed Jesus and His armies come out of Heaven riding horses: *"There before me was a **white horse**, whose rider is called Faithful and True...The armies of heaven were following him, riding on **white horses**"* (Revelation 19:11-14, NIV). And don't forget that Israel's great prophet Elisha also saw horses in the unseen realm (2 Kings 6:17).

WHAT ABOUT MY PETS?

I'm certain some of you are saying, "I don't really care if there's an eagle and a white horse in Heaven. What about my beloved pets? Will I see them again? And if so, do I have to wait until the resurrection of the dead? Is my dog or cat in Heaven now?"

When we look at the sum total of what the Bible says about God, man, and animals we can build a strong case that our furry and feathered friends are indeed waiting for us in the invisible Heaven. Note the following points:

One: Animals Have "Souls"

Individuals sometimes challenge the idea that pets go to Heaven by declaring that animals don't have souls. Therefore, when animals die, they're gone forever. But this is contrary to what God's Word tells us. The Genesis account of creation uses the same wording to describe both men and animals, revealing that just as men have an immaterial portion to their makeup, so do the creatures that inhabit this world.

When Almighty God created Adam, He first formed a physical body from the earth. Adam had no life, however, until the Lord *"breathed into his nostrils the breath of life; and man became a living soul"* (Genesis 2:7, KJV). Breath of life, in the original language, is the Hebrew word *chay*. Living soul is the Hebrew word *nephesh*, which refers to the non-material, invisible, inward portion in man. Both of these words are also used for animals in the Book of Genesis (Strong 2004). The first readers of the Scripture would have understood this to mean that animals have an immaterial portion to their makeup.

*"And God said, 'Let the water teem with **living creatures** [nephesh]'...So God created the great creatures of the sea and every **living** [nephesh] and moving thing with which the water teems"* (Genesis 1:20-21, NIV).

*"And God said, 'Let the land produce **living creatures** [nephesh] according to their kinds: livestock, creatures that move along the ground, and wild animals'"* (Genesis 1:24, NIV).

*"[God said], 'And to all the beasts of the earth and all the birds of the air and all the creatures that move on the ground—everything that has the **breath of life** [chay] in it—I give every green plant for food'"* (Genesis 1:30, NIV).

The Old Testament was translated into Greek in the third and second centuries before Christ. The men who made this first Hebrew-to-Greek translation used the Greek word *psuche* for the Hebrew word *nephesh. Psuche* refers to the seat of life itself or the portion that lasts beyond death (Strong 2004). When these scholars translated the above verses, they had no problem using a word for animals that was clearly understood to mean what you and I mean when we talk about a soul. If we study Church history, we find that the belief that animals have an immaterial part to their makeup dates back to the earliest days of Christianity and persisted until the AD 1600s and the Age of Enlightenment (see note 8).

Anyone who has lived in close contact with a pet, such as a dog or cat, is aware that they're more than mindless, soulless beasts who respond entirely by instinct. Animals display immaterial qualities like personality, intelligence, and emotions. We regularly hear stories in the news about pets who risk their own lives to save the lives of their human companions. The Bible even gives such an account. A donkey demonstrated courage, compassion, and loyalty when she saved her master from certain destruction. The passage records that the Lord opened the animal's mouth during the incident, and she articulated thoughts and feelings. There's nothing in the text that indicates this shouldn't be taken literally (Numbers 22:21-35).

Dead Like a Dog?

People sometimes misuse part of a statement in the Book of Ecclesiastes to try to prove that animals cease to exist when they die. Ecclesiastes is a record of one man's search for meaning and satisfaction along with a lament over the injustices and inequities of life. The author concludes with the realization that life without God is meaningless. He referenced animals to express the idea that men seem to have no advantage over them since everyone dies, man and beast alike.

> *"For that which befalls the sons of men befalls beasts, even one thing befalls them; as the one dies, so dies the other. Yes, they all have one breath and spirit, so that a man has no preeminence over a beast; for all is vanity—emptiness, falsity and futility! All go to one place; all are of the dust, and all turn to dust again"* (Ecclesiastes 3:19-20, AMP).

> *"Who knows the spirit of man whether it goes upward and the spirit of the beast whether it goes downward to the earth?"* (Ecclesiastes 3:21, AMP).

When the writer wrote these words, he wasn't making a theological comment on the eternal destiny of animals or lack thereof. His point is that no one escapes death. And he actually supports the idea that animals are more than mere physical bodies. Notice that the author used the same word (spirit) for humans and animals, acknowledging that both have an immaterial part or what we call a soul. As I've already stated, animals aren't created in the image of God nor are they equal with humans. However, they clearly have a non-human, immaterial portion to their makeup.

Two: It's Part of Continuity

There's continuity in our future—the same identity, the same earth, and the same cultures and civilizations. This pattern makes a strong case for the continuation of animals as well. The same animals that once lived on earth now live in Heaven and will one day live on the new earth.

Keep in mind that Almighty God fashioned all of creation to glorify Him. Animals, like us, are meant to praise and honor the Lord. It makes no sense that their entire created purpose is fulfilled for only the few short years they exist in this fallen world. It's in the life to come that all of us—men and animals—fully realize our destiny.

> *"Wild animals and all cattle, small creatures and flying birds, kings of the earth and all nations, you princes and all rulers on earth, young men and maidens, old men and children. Let them praise the name of the LORD, for his name alone is exalted; his splendor is above the earth and the heavens"* (Psalm 148:10-13, NIV).

> *"Let everything that has breath* [including animals] *praise the LORD"* (Psalm 150:6, NIV).

Three: God is a Good God

Our Savior Jesus said that God is a Father to His people, and He's better than the best earthly parent (Matthew 7:9-11). Why would the Lord make animals as companions or pets for His children and then allow us only a brief moment in time to enjoy them? When you consider the character of God, it's highly unlikely. No good father would be that cruel.

▸ ⇥⇥⇥▸ ∙ ◂⇤⇤⇤ ∙

Although there's no single verse that directly says animals go to Heaven, when we put all of these passages together, it's evident that our pets don't cease to exist at death. Their bodies return to dust as do ours. But they pass into the present Heaven to await reunion with their physical bodies and with us. We can look forward to being reunited with our beloved companions when we step into the unseen Heaven at death or when Jesus returns to earth, whichever happens first.

HEAVEN ON EARTH

*H*eaven is God's home, and even though it's in another dimension, the Lord has always intended to share this home with men. Redemption will culminate in the coming together of two dimensions when Heaven and earth unite to be the forever home of the Lord and His redeemed family. That's what the new earth will be—Heaven on earth. Allow me to explain.

PARADISE ON EARTH

To gain information about what's ahead, we must again look back to life on earth before sin. The opening pages of the Bible reveal that God and man walked and talked together in the Garden of Eden. The Genesis narrative draws the reader's attention to two trees in Eden—the tree of life and the tree of the knowledge of good and evil. The text informs us that the Lord God warned our first parents not to eat from the latter tree because they would die (Genesis 2:17). Adam and Eve disobeyed God and, through their disobedience, brought the curse of corruption and death to mankind and the earth (see note 9).

The forbidden tree is not mentioned again in the Scripture.

The tree of life, however, is mentioned two other times, and these references reveal that this unique tree is located in the unseen Heaven. Jesus referred to *"the tree of life, which is in the midst of the paradise of God"* (Revelation 2:7, KJV). The apostle John reported that he saw the tree of life in the capital city of Heaven (Revelation 22:1-2).

The fact that this tree was accessible to Adam and Eve indicates that the unseen dimension was initially open on earth. Heaven was visibly expressed in Eden. And although human beings are designed to live in a physical, material world, they could freely interact with the Invisible God in His dwelling place.

PARADISE LOST

When Adam and Eve sinned, the Garden of Eden closed to them and they were cut off from access to the tree of life. Mighty angelic beings, known as cherubims, were positioned to guard the Garden's entrance. The presence of these particular beings in Eden is another indication that Almighty God's home was open, and interaction between Heaven and earth prevailed before sin, since cherubims surround the throne of God in the invisible Heaven (Psalm 99:1; Isaiah 37:16).

> *"So the LORD God banished Adam and his wife from the Garden of Eden, and he sent Adam out to cultivate the ground from which he had been made. After banishing them from the garden, the LORD God stationed mighty angelic beings* [cherubims] *to the east of Eden. And a flaming sword flashed back and forth, guarding the way to the tree of life"* (Genesis 3:23-24, NLT).

Sometime thereafter, the Lord's home (Paradise or Heaven)

became not only inaccessible but also invisible to mankind.

PARADISE RESTORED

Two thousand years ago, the Lord Jesus Christ came out of the invisible Heaven into time and space to remedy this condition by paying for sin at the Cross. Our Redeemer restored access to God and His dwelling place for those who believe on Him: *"He died for sinners that he might bring us safely home to God"* (1 Peter 3:18, NLT).

Now, through faith in Christ and His death, burial, and resurrection, men and women can again live in Paradise. All who acknowledge Jesus as Savior and Lord pass into God's unseen home when they separate from their physical bodies at death. But the Lord's plan of redemption goes much further than this. Almighty God is going to recover all that was lost to sin, including unhindered interaction between the visible and invisible dimensions. The Lord never intended that there be a divide between these two realms. His intention was that the spiritual dimension be perfectly expressed through the physical. In connection with Jesus' return, the Lord will bring the seen and unseen realms together and God's home will once again be open to men on earth.

> *"Then when the time is right, God will do all that he has planned, and Christ will bring together everything in heaven and on earth"* (Ephesians 1:10, CEV).

This is the culmination of the plan of redemption—two separate realms coming together under the Lordship of Jesus Christ. Obviously, the thought of being able to freely interact with another dimension perfectly expressed through the one in which we presently live is beyond our comprehension right now. But God's Word gives enough information about the new earth to assure us that it will be wonderful, not strange or weird.

The Bible begins and ends with God on earth with His family, first in Eden with His man Adam and then with all His redeemed sons and daughters on the new earth. His home and our home will be one and the same—redemption completed.

› →››› · ‹‹‹← ‹

As we've worked our way through this study of our future, we've often referred to the apostle John and the information he received during his visit to Heaven. Here's one more thought. John saw the invisible dimension open up in this visible realm when he was shown the capital of Heaven descending to earth. The sight was so moving that he compared it to the breathtaking beauty of a bride coming to wed her husband.

> *"I saw the holy city, the new Jerusalem, descending from God out of Heaven, prepared as a bride dressed in beauty for her husband. Then I heard a great voice from the throne crying, 'See! The home of God is with men, and he will live among them. They shall be his people, and God himself shall be with them'"* (Revelation 21:2-3, J. B. Phillips).

John witnessed Heaven and earth come together to be the forever home of the Lord God and His family. When earth is made new, Almighty God's dwelling place will once again be accessible to men on earth—Paradise restored, Heaven on earth.

THE BEST IS YET TO COME

We all reach the point where there are more years behind us than ahead. The clock is running out. We must face the fact that many of our hopes and dreams aren't going to be realized and the losses and injustices we've experienced won't be undone. Not only is the aging process robbing us of the strength and vigor we once had, there's simply not enough time left. But the Bible gives us wonderful news. This life is not our only shot at life on earth. Therefore, we don't have to live with the pressure that if our goals aren't met and wrongs aren't righted before we die, it will never happen. Our greatest days are ahead, first in Heaven and then on the new earth when Heaven and earth are one and the same.

THIS LIFE FALLS SHORT

For most of the people born into this world since Adam and Eve, life has been filled with toil, pain, deprivation, and disappointment. Down through the centuries, humanity has faced disease, poverty, and famine along with the calamity generated by natural disasters and political upheaval. Many in the western world are fortunate enough to live in countries where relative peace, freedom, and prosperity prevail along with the

177

benefits of modern technology and medicine. Yet even though we have a better existence than most of the people who've ever lived on this planet, life is still challenging.

- We live with constant pressure and frustration. Most of us work at jobs we don't like. If you're lucky enough to be employed at a job you truly enjoy, you still have to deal with difficult bosses, unpleasant co-workers, endless paperwork, and needless government regulations.

- When we find time for pleasurable activities and amusements, they're often tainted by trials. Stinging jellyfish inundate the beach the week you get away to the seashore. Your weekend camping trip is marred by obnoxious neighbors in the next cabin. A relaxing summer vacation is overshadowed by the fact that you have to go back to work on Monday.

- Even when life is running smoothly, we know the phone can ring at any moment with devastating news that completely upends life as we know it.

- And none of this world's sophisticated technology can protect us from the pain generated by family dysfunction and breakup or the loss of a loved one to death.

Not only is life tenuous, many desires go unmet and numerous talents and abilities never bear fruit because of the harsh realities of life in a fallen world. The list of broken dreams, lost opportunities, and unused gifts is long.

- Since the beginning of time, multitudes of human beings have died without reaching adulthood and never realized their full potential.

- Countless millions had their destinies altered because they lived during a time of war, in a country with a cruel, despotic ruler, or in an empire where slavery prevailed.

- Imagine a gifted writer born a slave who didn't learn to write and never penned a word or a talented inventor who worked eighty hours a week to support his family and had no time to invent. Think about a tremendous athlete who couldn't play professional sports because his leg was severed in an accident or a beautiful singer who died of malaria in an impoverished country before her voice matured.

- How many people longed to marry but never found a spouse? How many others did marry but endured a miserable marriage? How many couples yearned for children but were unable to have them or lost a baby to miscarriage or a child to accident or disease? What about children who never knew the joy of a happy family due to abuse and neglect?

- And for those precious few who achieved their dreams and led mostly happy, prosperous lives, old age and death took it away.

The Lord never intended life to be like this. A close look at the Bible record reveals that the first thing God did following the creation of Adam, and mankind in Adam, was bless them.

> *"So God created man in his own image, in the image of God created he him; male and female created he them.* ***And God blessed them****"* (Genesis 1:27-28, KJV).

179

Among other things, to *bless* means "to make prosperous and happy" (Strong 2004). Almighty God's plan from the beginning was that His family would flourish with joyful contentment in the home He made for us. However, because of sin, corruption, and death, this hasn't been realized. If this life is our only chance at being continuously prosperous and happy on earth, then God's plan for man has been, and is, a dismal failure. Thankfully, that's not the case because the Lord's plan to bless humanity will be fulfilled. All will be made right in the life ahead. Redemption is big!

RESTORATION AND COMPENSATION

Although God provides for His own in this present life, the ultimate stage for the reversal of life's injustices, recompense for loss, and fulfillment of dreams and desires is ahead. In the life after this life, the Lord is going to redeem relationships, opportunities, and talents lost to life's hardships. Going to Heaven means more than the ending of suffering and pain. It means restoration and compensation.

- Jesus told His followers that the pains and wrongs of life will be reversed in Heaven. *"Blessed are you who hunger now, for **you will be satisfied**. Blessed are you who weep now, for **you will laugh**. Blessed are you when men hate you, when they exclude you and insult you and reject your name as evil, because of the Son of Man. Rejoice in that day and leap for joy, because **great is your reward in heaven"*** (Luke 6:21-23, NIV).

- The Lord assured His original twelve disciples that what they sacrificed to follow Him would be restored in His eternal kingdom. *"Everyone who has given up houses or brothers or sisters or father or mother or children or* *property, for my sake, **will receive a hundred times as much in return and will have eternal life**"* (Matthew 19: 29, NLT).

- The apostle Paul, in the context of the new earth, wrote, *"In my opinion whatever we have to go through now is less than nothing compared with **the magnificent future God has in store for us**"* (Romans 8:18, J. B. Phillips).

Losses Reversed, Opportunities Redeemed, Relationships Restored

Few people live with the knowledge that there's more to life than just this life. Therefore, when a young woman dies without marrying and raising a family or a father is killed and leaves behind small children, sorrow over the lost relationship is intensified by the lost opportunities. We lament that this father won't see his children grow up, and we grieve over what the young lady didn't get to experience. But if these two are in Heaven, they now live in a realm where there is no loss and all wrongs are made right.

Who are we to say that this young father knows nothing of his children's growth when the Bible reveals that people in Heaven are aware of some of the activity on earth?

- Shortly before Jesus was crucified, Moses and Elijah stepped out of the unseen realm to discuss with the Lord events about to transpire in Jerusalem (Luke 9:30-31). It's obvious these men were cognizant of what was happening on earth.

- Christians are instructed to live with the consciousness that *"we are surrounded by such a great cloud of witnesses* [people who have already gone to Heaven]" (Hebrews 12:1, NIV). This passage implies that those who've gone before us know about our progress.

- While John was in Heaven, he observed people praying for others still on earth (Revelation 6:9-10). They must have some knowledge of those they left behind in order to pray effectively.

I'm not suggesting that men and women in the unseen dimension contact and communicate with us. They don't (see note 4 and note 10). Neither am I saying that they watch our every move. I'm simply trying to help you see that there is no deprivation in going to Heaven. However it works, this father and the young woman will not lose out. They aren't lamenting what we think they missed out on by dying young. In the first place, both now have a different perspective and see things from the standpoint of eternity. Second, they've begun to experience some of the recompense of the life to come.

- The father recognizes that what seems to have been taken away from him and his children is nothing compared to what lies ahead if they all choose to follow him to Heaven. He knows they'll recover over and above what they temporarily lost.

- The young woman now has the emotional fulfillment we all want out of marriage but don't fully experience in this life. And she has relationships that meet her need to guide, nurture, and invest in someone else as she would have done had she borne children. Possibly, she's raising a child whose birth parents elected not to go to Heaven.

Let me be clear. I'm not minimizing the pain or the very real bereavement for those left behind when a friend or loved one dies. Rather, I want you to see the hope in the midst of grief. If you've been separated from someone you love by death, the knowledge that you'll one day be reunited and your relationship will pick up where it left off provides comfort as you grieve.

If your baby has died, that child is waiting for you, and you will have the opportunity to raise your son or daughter either in the present Heaven or on the new earth. How old will he or she be? Who cares for him or her until you arrive? We can't answer every question yet, but I think you're beginning to see that what's ahead is gain not loss (see note 11).

Yes, there are genuine separations and painful losses in this sin damaged world and many relationships end much too soon. *But it's all temporary!* The father referred to earlier will play with his children once more—even if they're old when they reach Heaven—because every trace of aging and corruption will be removed from them all. Imagine grandparents made youthful again running with their grandchildren for the first time. What old age and arthritis prevented them from doing in this life will be realized in our future home.

Maybe your loss came in the form of abandonment and abuse at the hands of your birth parents, and you've never known the blessing of a happy, nurturing family or had a parent you could trust. Those relational needs will be met in Heaven either through your family members perfected or through new people you'll meet.

LIFE AS IT'S MEANT TO BE

I recognize that I can't give specific Bible references for some of the points in this chapter. But these points make sense when considered in terms of the big picture. God's goal in redemption is the restoration of His purposes in creating humankind, along with the recovery of what was lost when man went astray. The Lord's aim is not to replace life on earth with something foreign to us but to restore it to what it was supposed to be.

Remember Continuity

Continuity has been a consistent theme throughout our study of Heaven: continuity of identity in God's family and continuity in the earth, the home the Lord made for His family. Life as we know it will carry on. The best of life in this fallen world gives us a glimpse of what's ahead. Every culture on earth since the beginning of time has relished the joys of family, feasts, and celebrations. This won't stop in the life to come.

Sadly, due to misinformation about Heaven, we fear we'll never again experience these cherished aspects of life. When a loved one dies, it's not uncommon to hear those left behind wistfully long for just one more Christmas, one more birthday, one more family holiday. I completely understand that sense of grief because I've experienced it myself. Yet there's hope in the midst of what is temporarily gone because we will celebrate with family and friends in the life to come. We will have another Christmas with them!

I've referred to the parable of the prodigal son a number of times. Jesus told the story to illustrate how Heaven responds when a wayward son comes home (Luke 15:11-32). The Lord described restoration of relationship between the father and his son as well as celebration over their reunion. The overjoyed dad threw a party to welcome back his boy. It was a gala event with music, dancing, food, drink, and guests—just what you and I think of when we envision a party. Jesus wouldn't have used this image to make His point unless joyful interaction between family and friends is part of our future. The Bible actually describes Almighty God Himself hosting a party for His family on the new earth.

> *"On this mountain the LORD Almighty will pre-*
> *pare a feast of rich food for all peoples, a banquet*
> *of aged wine...On this mountain he will destroy the*
> *shroud that enfolds all peoples, the sheet that covers*
> *all the nations; he will swallow up death forever. The*
> *Sovereign LORD will wipe away the tears from all*
> *faces"* (Isaiah 25:6-8, NIV).

The festivities that await us in the life to come will put to shame the best parties ever staged on this sin damaged earth. Can you envision the celebrations we'll have with family and friends when we're all perfected and every trace of corruption is gone? Imagine sitting down to a holiday meal where nobody gets drunk, and no screaming fights break out.

The Joy of Life

As wonderful as the good times can be in this present life, they're often tarnished by the realities of life in a fallen world. Even when life's pleasures meet our every expectation, the seeds of loss lie just below the surface because time is running out. We know it's too good to last. But that is going to change in our future home. The foreboding shadow of old age and death will be forever removed and the joy of life restored to us.

Everyone enjoys watching children play because it reminds us of the delight and wonder we had before we were old enough to know life's harsh realities. Each of us can recall the magic of childhood summers stretching endlessly before us.

We'd lie in the grass for hours watching clouds change shape in the midday sky. At night, we'd run with our friends and catch fireflies in a jar. That childlike spirit of zest for life, the elation and optimism that come from hope for the future—the joy of life—will be ours again.

NO NEED FOR A BUCKET LIST

Many people have a bucket list or a list of things they want to do and places they hope to visit before they die: see the Grand Canyon, go skydiving, climb Mount Everest, take a trip to Hawaii. Bucket lists come out of the belief that if you don't get something done in this life, you'll never get it done. Such thinking arises from a lack of understanding of the future. There's more to life than just this life, and many of our gifts, talents, passions, and interests aren't for this life but for the life to come. When you know this truth, it relieves the pressure as well as the sense of grief over what you know you won't achieve before time runs out.

I have a new earth list of things I intend to do and places I plan to visit when the earth is made new. At the top of my list is pursuing my passion for history. I've loved studying the past since I was a child but don't have the time or resources to follow this desire. I'll have that opportunity on the new earth. I'm going to travel to historical sites around the world. I look forward to meeting men and women who actually lived in the places and periods I'll explore. They can walk me through what happened at each site and give me details not found in the history books.

I've wanted to see long-ago events as far back as I can remember. I often stand at a spot and try to picture what it looked like in previous centuries. Because the Lord is not bound by time, I fully expect Him to permit me to see history as though I were there. I want to witness how God has worked in the affairs of men since time began and caused it all to serve His purposes. If you're a *Star Trek* fan, you're no doubt familiar with the holodeck on the starship Enterprise. It was a virtual reality system that enabled the crew to take a break from their duties, step back into the past, and actually experience it. Surely God's provision will surpass the imagination of the creator of this futuristic diversion.

Think about the father mentioned earlier in the chapter, the one separated from his babies by an early death. Once reunited, he and his grown children may opt to recreate those lost childhood years by stepping back in time. Whether you agree or not, here's my point: what's ahead is gain, not loss. Throw away your bucket list and start a new earth list!

On the new earth, you can pursue a passion, profession, or sport you had no time for in this life. Perhaps you'll write a great novel or compose a beautiful symphony as you utilize talents that lay dormant due to the circumstances of life. Maybe you'll be the first to walk on a planet at the edge of the solar system as you fulfill your previously unrealized, lifelong dream to travel through outer space.

› ❯❯❯❱ · ❰❰❰❰ ·

On this earth, when you're old, you can only look back— unless you know the Lord and understand your destiny. This life is not your only chance at life on earth. Life is not behind you. It's ahead of you. No one is going to look back at the old earth and lament, "If only I could...just one more time."

The clock is winding down, but don't be discouraged. There are no lost opportunities, just postponed ones. We have a future, not only in the present Heaven, but on the new earth as resurrected, fully perfected men and women forever young— living in and with time, not under the pressure that time is running out.

> *"The path of the righteous is like the light of dawn, that shines brighter and brighter until the full day"* (Proverbs 4:18, NASB).

CONCLUSION

Much of the focus in Christian circles today is on this life and making it all it can be with very little, if any, emphasis on our ultimate destiny. There's nothing wrong with trying to live the best life possible. But we must not overlook the fact that we're eternal beings and the greater part of our existence is after we leave this world. If this present life is the highlight of our existence, then we are sorry individuals. As the great apostle Paul wrote, *"If we have hope in Christ only for this life, we are the most miserable people in the world"* (1 Corinthians 15:19, NLT). Our perspective needs to change. What's ahead is not an afterlife. This is the *pre-life*.

Paul made another statement that bears repeating as we bring our study of Heaven to a close. *"Let heaven fill your thoughts; don't spend your time worrying about things down here"* (Colossians 3:2, TLB). There's such wisdom in his words. Life in a sin damaged world can be extremely challenging, but knowledge of what's to come provides hope and strength for the journey. The apostle also penned these words:

> *"For our present troubles are quite small and won't last very long* [in comparison to eternity]*...So we don't look at the troubles we can see right now; rather, we look forward to what we have not yet seen. For the troubles we see will soon be over, but the joys to come will last forever"* (2 Corinthians 4:17-18, NLT).

Misinformation about Heaven has robbed many of the joy of anticipating what's to come. These inaccuracies make our eternal home seem like loss rather than gain. If Jesus is your

Lord and Savior, you don't have to fear or dread life after this life. Our future is bright, first in the present invisible Heaven and then on the new earth when Heaven comes to earth. The new earth will be the earth we know and love—new but familiar, transformed but recognizable.

Our forever home won't be boring, freaky, or otherworldly. It will be what life was meant to be. God's purposes for man will be realized as we reach our full potential. His home will be our home and all that we do—whether at work or play—will glorify Him, bless our fellow man, and more than satisfy us.

We can't answer every question about what lies ahead. But let's not allow what we don't yet know undermine our confidence in or steal our excitement over what the Bible plainly reveals. *Heaven is gain, not loss, and the best is yet to come!*

THE WAY TO HEAVEN

Most of us consider ourselves to be good people. But the standard for how good we must be to enter Heaven is God Himself—and none of us measure up. *"For all have sinned; all fall short of God's glorious standard"* (Romans 3:23, NLT). We've broken God's Law and are guilty of sin before a holy God. Our sin has disqualified us from a future with the Lord in His home.

Jesus' sacrifice on the Cross is the only remedy for this condition. Jesus is more than a prophet or a good moral teacher. He is God become man without ceasing to be God. Two thousand years ago, He came out of eternity into time and space. The Lord took on human nature and went to the Cross to pay for sin so Heaven could once again be opened to men and women.

When we acknowledge Jesus Christ as our Savior and believe that His sacrifice paid the price for our sins, they are washed away. Accepting Jesus' sacrifice involves more than believing historical facts regarding His death and resurrection. It means that you bow your knee to Him as Lord and surrender your life to Him. If you give Almighty God your heart, mind, and soul (your entire being) in this life, He will give you unending life with Him, first in the present invisible Heaven and then on the new earth.

Life is precarious and no one is promised tomorrow. If you have never acknowledged Jesus as your Savior and Lord, I urge you to make this commitment to Him. Don't go out into eternity without Him. Jesus is the only way to Heaven.

NOTES

1. In 2 Corinthians 12:4, the apostle Paul reported that he *"heard inexpressible words, which a man is not permitted to speak"* (NASB). This passage is sometimes interpreted to mean the Lord doesn't want us to know anything about Heaven because Paul didn't speak about his experience. If that is true, then why was John directed to write a detailed account of his visit to Heaven in the Book of Revelation? Paul did not write about his experience for two reasons. First, while in Heaven, he heard things he was unable to find words to describe. Second, for reasons known only to God, the apostle was instructed not to disclose particular details about his trip to Heaven.

2. The Jerusalem Temple was actually based on an earlier structure called the Tabernacle. The Tabernacle was designed to be a place where the Lord could meet with His people as they worshipped and offered sacrifices. God gave Moses the specific instructions for building the Tabernacle when Moses went up on Mount Sinai to receive God's Law. The Lord told him, *"I want the people of Israel to build me a sacred residence where I can live among them. You must make this Tabernacle and its furnishings exactly according to the plans I will show you"* (Exodus 25:8-9, NLT). Paul later revealed that the pattern given to Moses was based on a structure in Heaven (Hebrews 8:5, 9:23).

3. People sometimes dismiss the account of the beggar and the rich man as merely a story rather than an actual event. But that can't be the case, because Jesus called one of the men Lazarus. In the many parables Jesus told, this is the only time He gave someone a name. The Lord had a close friend named Lazarus (John 11:5). It makes no sense that

He would choose this name for the beggar since it could easily be confused with His friend, unless it was the real name of an actual person.

According to Jesus, the fate of each man was very different and directly connected to his actions in life. The rich man went to Hell, a place of torment. Lazarus went to a place where he experienced the *"comforts and delights"* he missed out on in life (Luke 16:25, AMP). Jesus told this story as part of a response He gave to a group of religious leaders known as Pharisees. The Pharisees, like the rich man, were extremely greedy. Through His parable, the Lord warned these men of the consequences of their greed if they failed to respond to Almighty God.

Some aspects of Jesus' narrative require more explanation than we have space for in this book. But we can glean helpful information about what human beings are like in the unseen realm.

4. When people learn that men and women in the unseen realm are aware of activities on earth, this question frequently comes up: If our friends and loved ones know about our trials and tears, won't it take away from their joy? No, because people in Heaven have a different perspective. They see things from the standpoint of eternity and recognize that sufferings on earth are miniscule compared to the happiness of the life to come. It's similar to a parent whose child loses a favorite toy. Although the child is truly heartbroken, his mother and father know that in terms of an entire life span, the loss of a toy isn't as devastating as it seems to the youngster in the moment. The people in Heaven understand that life's hardships and pain are momentary in comparison to forever, so they aren't bothered by life's adversities in the

same way we are (2 Corinthians 4:17-18; Romans 8:18).

While John was in Heaven, he saw men and women crying out to God for those who were going to be martyred for their faith in Christ. Those people in Heaven did not pray, "Stop our brothers and sisters from being killed." Instead they prayed, "Lord, when will you carry out justice on earth and make things right?" They, along with the rest of Heaven's inhabitants, realize that God's ultimate goal is not to stop individual cases of temporary suffering and loss but to permanently restore mankind and the earth to what He intended before they were damaged by sin.

Do people in Heaven know if we get a new car or a job promotion? The Bible doesn't say. Rather, it indicates they are most concerned with our spiritual condition and Almighty God's unfolding plan of redemption (Luke 9:28-31; Hebrews 12:1).

5. To learn more about the fate of men and women who live in non-Christian countries and never hear the name of Jesus, go to our website (www.richesinchrist.com). You will find two in-depth audio teachings on this subject: *What About the Native in the Jungle* (October 4, 2013) *and More About the Native in the Jungle* (October 11, 2013).

6. The Old Testament prophets weren't given every detail about the events that transpire in connection with the establishment of God's eternal kingdom on earth. Consequently, a single prophecy may include several events that are separated by many years. For example, Isaiah wrote, *"For unto us a child is born, unto us a son is given: and the government shall be upon his shoulder"* (Isaiah 9:6, KJV). The beginning of his prophecy describes Jesus' first coming as a baby born to

Mary in Bethlehem. But the second part refers to something He will do as part of His Second Coming—take control of the government of earth.

There are different stages to the Lord's return, as well as events that unfold over a period of time (the rapture, the tribulation, various judgments, the millennial kingdom). These are topics for another book. Our present goal is to examine the end result—the new heavens and the new earth. The verses I cite to describe life on the new earth are located in passages that also include other aspects of the Lord's return. Hopefully, this note will allay any confusion that may arise if you've heard these verses applied to specific end-time events other than the new earth. There is overlap in these passages.

7. The following is a quote from an article in *Acts and Facts*, a monthly publication from the Institute for Creation Research: "Over the years, creation thinkers have evaluated many pre-Flood possibilities. For example, the old ICR model of a vapor canopy capping Earth's atmosphere has not performed well under rigorous modeling tests. Until new information arrives, we should not insist on detailed reconstructions of the pre-Flood world, but we can continue to investigate that intriguing time with a little science and a lot of Genesis" (Thomas Jan 2016, p. 20).

8. As more evidence that the first Christians believed animals possess an immaterial part to their makeup, notice how the New Testament writers used the word *psuche* in a familiar passage of the Scripture. This verse was written only a few years after Jesus returned to Heaven. Each word in bold print is *psuche* in the original Greek text. *"For whosoever will save his **life** shall lose it: and whosoever will lose his*

life for my sake shall find it. For what is a man profited, if he shall gain the whole world, and lose his own soul? or what shall a man give in exchange for his soul" (Matthew 16:25-26, KJV).

9. Questions may arise as to what kinds of trees the tree of life and the tree of the knowledge of good and evil were, as well as their purpose. The Bible doesn't say what types of trees they were. As to their purpose, space doesn't permit a detailed discussion, but consider one thought. Although both were actual trees, they were also symbolic. Had Adam eaten from the tree of life, it would have been an expression of submission to and dependence on the Lord. This choice would have united Adam (and man in Adam) to the eternal life in God. Eating from the other tree was a choice toward independence from the Lord. It resulted in death for Adam and the human race because it separated mankind from the only source of life, Almighty God.

10. The fact that Moses and Elijah talked with Jesus is not evidence that human beings in the unseen realm communicate with people on earth. This event was a unique situation. These two Old Testament saints came to talk with Jesus, who was and is God Incarnate (or God in human flesh). They said nothing to Peter, James, or John. Both Moses and Elijah played significant roles in God's unfolding plan of redemption during their lifetimes. The crucifixion was a key event in that plan, and these men were given the privilege of consulting with the Lord shortly before it took place.

11. Can we be certain that babies and young children go to Heaven? A detailed discussion of this issue would fill another book. But consider some brief thoughts. There is no one Bible verse that directly says infants and children

do or don't go to Heaven. But God's Word gives us several strong clues. Scripture informs us that when King David's infant son died, this grieving father was comforted by the knowledge that he would see his baby again in the life to come (2 Samuel 12:23).

God is a just God who does right by every human being, including those who die before they are old enough to acknowledge the good news of salvation through Jesus Christ. As we've discussed throughout our study of Heaven, Almighty God's plan is not the destruction but the recovery and redemption of what He created in the beginning. The Bible declares that through His death and resurrection, Jesus provided much more for mankind than Adam's sin took from God's creation (Romans 5:12-19). Based on the Lord's character and His purpose in redemption, we can rest assured that, somehow, there is provision for babies and little children through the Cross.

BIBLIOGRAPHY

Missler, Chuck, and Mark Eastman. 2013. *Alien Encounters: The Secret Behind the UFO Phenomenon.* Coeur d'Alene, ID: Koinonia House, pp. 85-87.

Strong, James. 2004. *Strong's Complete Word Study Concordance: Expanded Edition.* Edited by Warren Baker. Chattanooga, TN: AMG Publishers.

Thomas, Brian. 2016. "Creation Q & A: What Was the Pre-Flood World Like?" *Acts & Facts*, January, p. 20.

Vine, W. E. 1984. *The Expanded Vine's Expository Dictionary of New Testament Words.* Edited by John R. Kohlenberger. Minneapolis, MN: Bethany House Publishers.

Webster's New Students Dictionary. 1969. Springfield, MA: G & C Merriam Co.